Sacrifice

an affair to remember...

BARBARA HARKNESS

Copyright © 2021 by Barbara Harkness

All rights reserved. No part of this book may be used or reproduced by any means, graphic, electronic, or mechanical, including photocopying, recording, taping or by any information storage retrieval system without the written permission of the publisher except in the case of brief quotations embodied in critical articles and reviews - without written consent from Barbara Harkness.

Cover image © Barbara Harkness

This book is an autobiographic memoir – the names of some people have been changed to protect their identity. As the author of this work I (Barbara Harkness) acknowledge the moral rights have been asserted with the copyright, designs and patents act 1968. If you wish to use any of my material you may contact me for permission. All rights reserved.

www.barbaraharkness.com
Cover design and text layout designed by Barbara Harkness ©
Photographs taken by Barbara Harkness ©
First published 2014 by DoctorZed Publishing.
Second edition 2022 Published by Life IS Art Publishing

ISBN: 978-0-6456712-2-3 print
ISBN: 978-0-6456712-3-0 ebook

For Michael

CARPE DIEM

You can connect from all kinds of places- energetic harmony, sexual alchemy, intellectual alignment- but they won't sustain love over a lifetime. You need a thread that goes deeper, that moves below and beyond the shifting sands of compatibility. That thread is fascination- a genuine fascination with someone's inner world, the way they organize reality, the way they hearticulate their feelings, the unfathomable and bottomless depths of their being. To hear their soul cry out to you again and again, and to never lose interest in what it is trying to convey. If there is that, then there will still be love when the body sickens, when the sexuality fades, when the perfection projection is long shattered. If there is that, you will swim in love's waters until the very last breath.

-Jeff Brown

(~an excerpt from 'An Uncommon Bond', available at any bookstore through Ingram Distribution, and on Amazon at http://www.amazon.com/gp/product/0980885957/)

Sacrifice
an affair to remember...

BARBARA HARKNESS

BOOK ONE

PUBLISHED BY

Life is ART

*If you believe that everything happens for a reason,
that simple life lessons and deep emotional insights
are gifts we can share with others,
then this book is for you.*

BARBARA HARKNESS

*And it's no sacrifice, just a simple word,
it's two hearts living in two separate worlds.
But it's no sacrifice, no sacrifice,
it's no sacrifice at all.*

WORDS BY ELTON JOHN

INTRODUCTION - page 9

***

CHAPTER 1 - page 13
Temptation

***

CHAPTER 2 - page 67
Two Separate Worlds

***

CHAPTER 3 page 119
Negativity Lands

***

CHAPTER 4 - page 145
We Lose Direction

***

CHAPTER 5 - page 195
The Final Act

***

EPILOGUE + AUTHORS NOTE - page 252

*To embark on the journey,
one must first be prepared...
...to lose sight of the shore.*

Anon

INTRODUCTION

Is love something we hope to find some day? Or do we chain and lock our dreams of love away, our fears and insecurities forbidding access to our genuine selves, like chastity belts of the soul?

Do we give little bits of it away along our life's path, leaving crumbs with each person, who will not remember the love for the bite was not big or tasty enough?

Are we so diminished by our first heartbreak that love gets exiled to damnation for giving so much away?

Is a soul-mate a person who is so perfect for you that they reflect your very essence? A partner who blends into your life with as little resistance as possible? The concept of soul-mates can smack of co-dependency, in a certain light. But there are couples who do seem to go the distance as if destined to do so; those at eighty-five, walking along hand-in-hand. Perhaps their hands have never held those of another. It has been known that such couples often die within just a few months of one another. Can each of us find that soul-mate?

Throughout our lifetime we will undoubtedly experience more than one intimate relationship and each combination of relationship is unique in itself. When another person awakens in our deepest selves a desire and longing to connect, I call it a *'soul connection.'* In soul connections, physical contact is irrelevant. The mutual feelings are so strongly embedded there is no need to express them physically, because the connection is a part of the fabric of the universe; it wasn't created when you met, and it is not destroyed if you part.

Relationships should also offer the space in which we can experience ourselves as we truly are and enable us to fulfil our true potential. Sure, lasting relationships probably are about common interests and backgrounds. But at a soul level it is also about experiencing a person that brings out that intrinsic nature lying dormant in you; the opposite, an enigma that we find so attractive in another person, is often a place we have never visited within ourselves before and that person brings the gift of life itself.

If we are lucky enough, a special person might come along and rattle our cage more than another. They may even go down in our own personal history of love as being our soul-mate, or *'The One.'* The One that infuses you with a lustful appetite for life, that makes your spirits soar, who calms your psyche and reignites your creativity. The One who, ultimately, makes you question your beliefs and thus allows you to grow as a person and as a soul.

Reflecting upon my marriage and the simple fact that I had married far too young and now needed to experience other aspects of myself; it was only upon leaving the marriage that I had the room and freedom to grow and start the long process of accepting myself again, to reinvent myself, to reclaim my youth and the vibrancy of being a beautiful young woman. I had followed my instinctive female intuition when I realized that I could no longer remain in a marriage which offered no recourse to spiritual or personal growth. I left my family; I sacrificed motherhood to find myself once more and have lived with my guilty heart every day since. That's something I deal with personally to this day, because mothers never stop loving their children. That love never leaves.

Sacrifice is the story of my heart's awakening to love again; a validation to the magic we can create in our lives and how we attract exactly what we need when we are tuned in to the cosmic

Sacrifice

plane that runs parallel to our lives. I experienced the cosmic plane when I was open to its gifts, and I believe we all have this ability to connect with our inner superior consciousness.

The future is an exciting place.
It is not a place we are going,
it is a place we are creating.
The paths to it are not found,
they are made,
and the act of making them.....
changes both the creator,
and the destination.

Anon

CHAPTER 1

Temptation

[Paris - Bordeaux - Taormina - London / June - 1995]

Michael entered the foyer of the Timotel Gare de Nord wearing a yellow shirt, denim jeans and loafers. His height and deep voice caught my instant attention, but I did not remember him looking this attractive. His hair was longer (and sexier) than I'd remembered. I'm five-foot-nothing in heels; Michael, at six feet four inches, made him a relative skyscraper. I felt nearly insignificant as he welcomed me with his arms wide open.

As we embraced, he said, "Barbara, have you been waiting long? It's so very lovely to see you again."

I was transfixed by his sensual voice and the way he said my name—his tone, his British accent—I was lost.

It suddenly occurred to me: It couldn't be Michael, could it? Is he the One? I cannot say why but I had a gut feeling that the holiday I had embarked upon would be life-changing, owing to the intuitive feeling that I would have a romantic liaison of some sort.

"To go, or not to go?" had been my dilemma. Why is it that so many women need to flee their homeland and search for enlightenment after the end of a marriage or relationship? In my case, it was to Europe that I fled. Naturally, I made my first stop in Paris. I suppose I thought that going to the motherland of my lineage would somehow offer up the answers to life I so desperately craved.

Perhaps I should have ventured out into the big wide world

like many young adults in their early twenties. Instead, I had only managed to escape across the ditch like every other New Zealander, to the land of opportunity—Australia—at the tender young age of seventeen. I met my future husband within months of my arrival. Now I was at the ripe young age of thirty-eight, finally heading out alone for my European adventure.

There were times when I very nearly cancelled my trip for financial reasons. I was in the middle of building a new townhouse and I did not exactly relish the idea of traveling alone.

But in the end, I thought to myself, *I need to do this, let's see what life is like on the other side of the world.*

I wanted to explore new places and have new experiences after closing the door on my marriage. The words *"Be careful what you wish for"* never rang so true as they did for me in the following eighteen months. I didn't know it then, as I boarded the Air France flight to Charles de Gaul, but I was about to become the writer, director and semi-tragic femme fatale of my own play.

I thought Paris to be a likely place for a romantic liaison, and I was certainly ready for one. My search began on arrival. I must have had some kind of pick-up radar because no sooner had I stepped outside the Timotel Gare de Nord than I was followed by a good-looking Frenchman in a trench coat. He'd made it obvious with his double-take upon seeing me, and then sauntering close behind me as I walked. Mind you, the men in Paris all look pretty women right in the eye and it always means what it feels like it means: *"I want you."* There were no language barriers between the Frenchmen and me. It seemed as though every single man was saying, *"Well I'm up for it, are you?"* He followed me for a while and finally caught up and invited me to have coffee with him.

The Frenchman was drop-dead gorgeous: tall, dark, hand-

Sacrifice

some, and self-possessed. I loved his accent but interpreting what he was saying without having mastered French meant delving into my French translator for appropriate phrases. These did not really do the conversation any justice, let alone open the channels for flirting. After half an hour of hand gestures and one-word sentences, we both knew the short affair was doomed and went our separate ways. We parted with wry smiles. We knew what might have been.

And what a nice way to start the day, I thought, having coffee with a complete (and gorgeous) stranger.

French men are so very attractive and accommodating (and quite possibly extremely vain) and so I decided to capture them with my camera instead. It proved to be a great conver-sation-starter for as soon as they discovered I was a tourist, they'd be easily persuaded to pose for photographs. This is how I found a willing tour guide for a day; Jacques, who wanted to practice his English, and I, my French. He drove the trains on the Paris Metro and gave me a wonderful tour of the city by rail. It was nice to have company, albeit with limited communication, and despite not having much in common. His idea of having a good time was being parked in front of his video entertainment system watching a Monty Python movie in French with English subtitles, and his idea of French cuisine was lunch at Pizza Hut. I'd asked him if we could go to an authentic French Restaurant to experience what France was renowned for—its cuisine—my treat. But sadly his comprehension of the English language was as good as my comprehension of French, and he must have interpreted this as *your* favorite restaurant, because we ended up at Le Pizza Hut.

***

To my surprise, traveling alone felt pretty good, though the language barrier was proving tough. I decided to give up exploring French men after Jacques. I would simply play the tourist. For four days I walked the streets of Paris in awe of its majesty, loving the contrast which is so apparent between a European country and Australia. I drank in the culture of Paris as I wandered her streets, making stops along the way at the numerous patisseries for refueling on coffee and something sweet and delicious. Visiting along the way all the obligatory tourist attractions; Eiffel Tower, Pompidou Centre, Montmarte, Arc de Triomphe, Notre Dame, and finally drowning in the art at the Louvre.

By the time my four days of cultural immersion in Paris were up, I was looking forward to traveling south to attend Vinexpo, a four-day event held biannually in Bordeaux. I needed good wine and some company.

I was the new kid on the block in the wine industry, work-ing as a wine label design consultant to family vignerons in Australia who were beginning to market their own vintages. The wine industry is predominantly masculine, so being a young woman in this male-oriented domain had its benefits. Word had it that I was *a breath of fresh air,* and so the grapevine effect worked very well for my new business. I seemed to be doing all the right things as far as branding was concerned, and the business had flourished to the point where I could take myself off on these overseas jaunts and enjoy the fruits of my labour. I loved the way the industry had taken me in and lauded me as a rising star, and I loved the social connections that made the wine industry flow the way it did. This was the mid 90s, however, when Australian wine had begun to gain a strong and loyal following in Europe. Australian vintners were finally making money from their enterprises, and

Sacrifice

spend it they did. The Australian wine industry was full of so many rising stars, and they all liked to splash their new found fortunes around with expensive dinners to endorse how well they were doing. I often refer to the 90s of the Australian Wine Industry as the hedonistic days; parties, dinners, events galore. Though I will not miss another blind wine tasting with the sock or paper bag covering the bottle as long as I live!

Many of my clients had expressed that Vinexpo was *the event* to attend for networking, that the mile long pavilions would provide an abundance of credible inspiration for my work. Attending was an excuse to socialize and network and have a holiday on my company's expense.

***

Michael collected my bags, holding doors like a gentleman as we headed for his stylish Audi waiting at the curb. I thought to myself: *Nice work, girl. Way to go!* By the time we had skirted the perimeter of Paris and the niceties of polite conversation, I was starting to glance across at him trying to take in his appearance. Nice nose, lips good, I thought. Looks like he's been working out too, mmm... He had nice abs, and a receding hairline that I overlooked because he was obviously making up for it in length. I was instantly attracted to him, and yet I knew virtually nothing about him.

He was surprised to hear that I had been married and had two teenage boys. I was also surprised to discover that he was married with children, because he exuded a very high availability factor. It has always amazed me how some married men can so easily disguise the fact that they are indeed, well, married. Regardless of Michael's marital status, It was wonderful to be in the company of someone who spoke English after five days of trying to communicate with Parisians. Foreign countries are fun, but there comes a time when playing charades becomes just a little tiresome and frustrating.

I had met Michael on two other separate occasions during his annual company visits to Adelaide for business. He was merely a business acquaintance. We'd had a small amount of correspondence prior to my arrival in Europe, through faxes, and he had very kindly offered some invaluable advice on how to get around Paris and certain things to avoid (like French men). The accommodation in Bordeaux had been pre-arranged by Michael for the entire Australian contingent, which, as it turned out, was me.

As we travelled farther south on the auto route A10 towards Bordeaux, we both revealed more about ourselves than was politically correct. Of course, his admission that he felt he had married for all the wrong reasons made it blatantly clear that he was in an unsatisfactory relationship, and it became the focal point of discussion for most of the remaining week. We also talked more broadly. He felt the world had become a very selfish place, full of people servicing their own needs instead of putting others before themselves.

"Well, how are you going to make others happy when you are not happy yourself?" I asked as we sped through the French countryside.

He sensed my discomfort over the differing views. He was British, after all, and admitted that his schooling and upbringing had brought about certain conditionings that taxed any normal person's psyche beyond reasonable limits. I told him in response that I had thrown out the old rule book and was making up better rules as I went along. I abide by the rules that make you happy

Sacrifice

and are fair to those around me. He seemed to like that idea. I could tell he was taking in most of what I was saying.

Again I looked over at him to observe his handsome profile, and thought, *mmm, pity he's married,* because one of my *rules* was: No married men! It was a long drive to Bordeaux, some five hours, so there was plenty of time to ponder that particular rule, or not!

"The truth is something we carry with us through our lives," I began very carefully. "Unfortunately for some, this turns into a lie, and the personal deceit we carry with us gnaws away at our soul. This was how I'd felt in my marriage, like a caged animal yearning to be free. I had all the trappings of a successful life, but they were just that, trappings. A six-bedroom home, two cars in the garage, swimming pool, private school education for the children. While society puts value on these outward signs of success, and common sense dictates being happy with what we have, then why was I so darned unhappy with all the wonderful stuff I had?"

"Had you fallen out of love with your husband?" he asked.

"I still loved him, but I wasn't in love with him. I had a pervasive feeling that I had become a fraud. I simply did not want to play this wife-and-mother role any more. I wanted to be someone else. Quite possibly the University environment I had been inducted into as a mature-age student had altered my personal perspective, opened up other opportunities and therefore changed my life's course. I wanted to find out who I really was in the solitude of my own space without the demands of a family. If I had stayed and lived that lie—my life—according to society's expectations and social values, I would have shriveled and died inside. I had already felt the decay of my soul. I felt that I was a commodity in my family, serving everyone else's needs and meeting their requirements, with no-one, including me, ever caring to wonder about my needs."

He became very quiet. I knew I'd hit a nerve, so I put a lid on it. Don't go there, I told myself. But I could tell he was at the same place that I had been not so long ago.

We stopped for lunch at the small town of Cognac around 2pm. Michael had lived and worked here in 1972, having been affiliated with the wine industry all his working life, and spoke French eloquently. Being the avid rugby fan that he was, we looked for a pub with a television because the English were, ironically, playing the New Zealand All Blacks in the semi-finals of the Rugby World Cup. The pub progressively filled with acquaintances of Michael's from the wine trade, also en route for Vinexpo. I was cheering for the All Blacks, of course.

As I cheered for the All Blacks in that little pub in the French countryside with a bunch of rowdy Brits and meek Frenchmen in berets watching on in amusement, Michael's leg ever so lightly touching mine, I became aware that something magic was happening between us. The rugby game and pub frivolities were secondary to the heightened sense of familiarity developing between us, and I knew he sensed it too.

***

We arrived in Bordeaux late afternoon and went straight to the Vinexpo pavilion to drop off boxes of Aussie wine. Michael had organized five days in a guest house in Le Bouscat, an outer suburb of Bordeaux, for ourselves and another client from the trade. We arrived at the accommodation, which was fenced by eight-foot walls and massive foreboding iron gates. We looked at each other anxiously. Michael pressed the buzzer and the gates

Sacrifice

opened to reveal a stunning, exquisite house. We both sighed with relief. In contrast to the surroundings, this estate was an oasis of lush greenery set on half an acre of land. Its long gravel driveway lead to a glorious wood-clad Hamptons style house, which had a veranda fronting on to a perfectly manicured lawn that was surrounded by a high hedge of cypress pines.

Madame came out to greet us and I was extremely thankful Michael spoke fluent French. She showed us to our rooms on the upper level, which had been allocated for guest accommodation. There were three rooms, each painted a different soft pastel color in French wash, with white painted beams and seagrass matting on the floor. All the rooms had shuttered windows which faced onto the magnificent grounds. My first impression was that Madame had impeccable taste; each room had fresh flower arrangements and ornaments perfectly chosen and placed in just the right way that seemingly only the French do without any contrived effort. My senses were overcome by the beauty around me. The smell of exotic garden plants and fresh cut grass wafting up through the open windows made me dizzy with joy—or was it something else?

Michael chose the aqua blue bedroom. I chose the pink one. There was a yellow bedroom in between, which was left for the another guest from Germany who was to join us later that evening.

I could not help but push the pause button on this picture-perfect scene to reflect on where I had been and how far I had come since the end of my marriage a mere eighteen months ago. I had been through very lonely times, even wondering if I had made the right decision to exit the marriage. Married at eighteen, I was a young mother of two fine boys by the time I was twenty-three years old. My twenties had consisted of traveling to remote outback Australian towns with my husband, (a mining engineer) and our small children. Don't get me wrong, we had been very happy with this lifestyle and I loved every aspect of not knowing where we would live next. My life had an unpredictability that I liked. Being able to set up camp wherever the work took us meant we had a new adventure to look forward to every couple of years, and I was good at traveling light without the encumbrances of a traditional family home.

The remote locations also offered something else, a vast exotic and ever-changing visual backdrop for my burgeoning talent as a painter. Without the interruptions of our extended family or the distraction of friends, I took up oil painting, which I relished and developed with zeal. I sometimes wondered upon reflection if finally settling in the burbs after the roaming years and the conformity it brought to our existence was the downfall of our marriage. Now, in France, I felt I was experiencing the life I had only dreamed about, and the feeling that I was creating that dream flowed through every fibre of my body.

***

That evening Michael and I took a walk. The air was balmy and the evening light lingered deliciously, adding another dimension to what was turning out to be a perfect day. We collected meats, cheeses and a loaf of French bread from the local delicatessen for our supper. We heartily enjoyed our picnic on the veranda overlooking the garden, washed down with a 1985 Bordeaux to complement the perfect setting.

Madame and her husband were not at home; we were completely alone. The chemistry between us was charged with anticipation of what the rest of the evening might bring, only to be defused when the other guest arrived. Marcel was a wine retailer from Germany and a business associate of Michael's. His voice was loud which I found irritating and the total antidote to an otherwise perfectly romantic evening. He added a touch of comedy, however, for we laughed and joked endlessly about him all week long as we tried our hardest to avoid him at every turn.

After clearing away the food, I went upstairs. I was not at all surprised to find Michael in my room when I opened the door. He was standing at the window, arms folded, waiting with an air of certainty.

"I thought you may need some instruction on how to work these shutters," he said.

"Show me," I replied.

It was a relatively easy exercise to pull them shut and close the latch, but with that lesson out of the way we proceeded to the next...our first kiss.

"I've wanted to taste you all day, Barbara."

My head was spinning and I needed to consider the consequences of what might happen. As if I could really stop it! In my heart I felt this was not going to be just an affair or holiday romance. But my revised rules met a second challenge. Namely, if Michael and I were going to make love I'd have to seriously reconsider Rule #2: Don't bonk the client!

Marcel appeared at the doorway just then, wanting Michael to show him how the shutters worked in his room. Michael and I looked at each other in a way that acknowledged we could have quite easily have made love that first night. I sent him away to help Marcel with his shutters, and before that kiss could become anything more serious.

***

At breakfast the next day, I tried to readjust my priorities and said to myself, *Don't fall for this guy! Besides being married, and a client, he's going bald and grey and for Christ's sake he's wearing a pink shirt and a tie with little kangaroos all over it to impress you! Get a grip, girl!* But I looked into his eyes and saw love and kindness.

I set out that morning on my own to see some of Bordeaux, do some shopping and try to calm my emotions a little. I planned to go to Vinexpo in the afternoon. Marcel had already gone to the expo with Michael and had kindly loaned me his car. BIG mistake! It never occurred to me how difficult it would be to drive sitting on the left side of a car, change gears with my right hand, remember the windshield wipers were not the turn indicators and vice versa, concentrate at being on the right hand side of the road, all while navigating my way into a new town!

I was a blithering mess by the time I found a car park, and seriously considered abandoning the vehicle and telling Marcel that it had been stolen. Perhaps I should have, for I also got lost trying to find Vinexpo in the afternoon. At one point I had the conference hall within my sights from the freeway, only to take the wrong exit and be carried away in the opposite direction with the flow of traffic. I think I drove around for three hours, just hoping I would spot the hall again. I also wished I'd learned more French, for when I did stop to ask for directions, all I could say was, "Vinexpo?" In reply, the locals could only point in an approximate direction.

When I finally arrived, exhausted from my harrowing European motoring experience, I headed straight for the Australian stand, racing past the wonderful label exhibits and ready to give Michael anything he wanted in exchange for a lift back to the lovely house at Le Bouscat. In retrospect, perhaps a large part

Sacrifice

of the reason I had lost my way was because I could think of nothing else but seeing him again and being in his company all day.

That evening we travelled into the center of Bordeaux for dinner in the lively Saint Pierre district, the historic Place du Parlement. I was in awe of Michael's ability to drive and navigate the freeways and roads simultaneously. He had been to Bordeaux on many other occasions and knew the area relatively well. I of course was still recovering from my earlier driving experience and was grateful to be in the passenger seat. Place du Parlement was a delight to behold, a piazza flooded with restaurants, every establishment overflowing with acquaintances from the wine trade. Even though the night was warm, Michael suggested we sit inside, away from prying eyes.

Chez Edouard was a typical French restaurant with rattan chairs and the obligatory crisp white table cloth. The menu did not seem to matter, so I asked if Michael would order me something very French—a surprise. Although when the meal arrived, the traditional snails in garlic were not really a surprise, as they were standard fare on any menu in Sydney during the 70s. Regardless, I was thankful that we were not at Le Pizza Hut. We might as well have been, for neither of us were too interested in the food. Even the crème bruleé, which was sublime, went uncredited owing to our complete immersion in one another.

It transpired that Michael had been looking forward to getting to know me for quite some time. Had our first meeting, two years prior in my Adelaide office, evolved into this magical moment in which we found ourselves? I have always believed that everything happens for a reason, and now I had the unmistakable feeling that the Universe was conspiring in our favor, that our meeting had occurred by more than pure chance.

At this point in his life, Michael was questioning a lot about himself and where he wanted to be. Call it mid-life crisis, a turning point, navel gazing, or whatever you choose. It is a time when we ask questions of ourselves. When an honest answer can't be found, we are in trouble. I was a sympathetic listener, and in light of what I had recently been through myself, was able to provide some insight to some of his problems. I was the teacher and he the willing student, for he seemed to devour my advice and opinions like food for his hungry soul.

"What made you leave in the end?" he asked.

"Well it was just this 'thing' inside me. It kept me awake at three in the morning and tapped at my subconscious continually throughout the day. The voice deep inside just kept saying, *'You have to leave!'* I'd talk myself out of it for an awfully long time, justifying the fact that I had a good husband and two gorgeous boys. Until one day, I had a conversation with my husband and suggested that we visit a marriage counsellor. He was against it and thought it to be a passing phase, like all the arguments. He felt so confident in his ability as a provider and the fact that the eighteen year-old girl he'd married could not possibly survive on her own, that she wouldn't leave. Well, I did go to the counsellor, on my own and poured my heart out to him, along with a flood of tears. I painted my picture-perfect life to him as best I could, along with the inner conflict of searching for my identity. But at the end of the session, during which he let me do all the talking, I said, "So, what's wrong with me?"

His response was a defining moment in my life. It was all I needed to take the plunge. He was the validation I needed, a professional person totally removed from my life who did not know either of us, and he simply said, "It's okay. We are sometimes here to help people move on, not necessarily to stay."

Sacrifice

Someone had finally understood me, seen my real life. I had portrayed my pain and anxiety of denying the truth and in an instant I was glad my husband had refused to attend. I wondered, if he had come with me, whether the outcome of the session would have helped us stay together.

Michael responded, "Do you regret not trying harder, for the sake of the children, at the very least?"

"Oh look, I am not absolving myself of my own part in the end of my marriage, and leaving my children was by far the hardest aspect of the separation, but I made sure that I did not move too far away and made it very clear that they were welcome in my new home and could visit me whenever they liked. My eldest son stopped talking to me, but I discovered later this was because his father was downloading his grief onto him every night. He took his father's pain on, which resulted in resenting me terribly."

"But when I told my youngest that I was leaving he just said, *'I know you're unhappy mum and I just want you to be happy again.'*

"Now that's what I call unconditional love!" I went on, and looked at Michael with a certainty and conviction in what I had said. "Because mothers don't normally leave their children, do they? But he also understood that it was my truth."

I paused for a minute, carefully reflecting on what I had to say because I knew Michael would take in everything I was telling him.

"The truth is what drives us", I said. "It's what makes you want to get out of bed every morning and face each day knowing that you are on your life's path. We all have one, finding it is a bit like walking through a quagmire at times but it is there waiting for each of us. Unfortunately, the truth unsettles our psyche every now and then as well. Some of us stumble and fall, or wander off the path for a while, but getting back onto it is part of the journey, and at the end we can say quietly to ourselves, *'I led a good life, the best I could, and I know it was an honest life. I was true to myself in every way.'* Imagine arriving at the end of your journey and on your deathbed felt that your whole life was a great big fat lie. Well it's too late then, isn't it?"

He just looked at me in acknowledgement, and said, "You're very brave. I admire you."

I smiled, grateful for his kind words, but said, "Nothing brave about it, Michael, it was the hardest thing I'll ever do in my whole life. It was difficult to hurt people I love for my own selfishness, but the other path would have been a total compromise and unhappiness for us all."

I had the feeling that Michael was on his own search for enlightenment. His life, it seemed, had been reduced to function only and had lost all meaning for him. He had lived his entire life by the rule book, without question, in true British stiff upper-lip-style, keeping up appearances no matter what. In holding true to the life he had created, had come to realize that he felt like a fraud, and that the only person he was deceiving was himself.

I did not always give him the answers he wanted to hear. In fact, when talking of his relationship with his wife, I would more often empathize with her feelings to help Michael see marriage from a woman's perspective, and this helped him to understand some of her actions which he had found confusing. From my own experience, when it came to the end of a marriage, there usually is no way of sorting it out; it is the end and should really be looked upon as a whole new beginning.

Alas, there is so much debriefing involved that what often results is blame and resentment. So often a divorce is no one's fault. Was this trauma the unnecessary result of society emphasizing

Sacrifice

the opinions of other family members and traditional religious values over and above our own opinions and values? I only wish societies values could help couples who had come to the end of the road and not shun them for being failures. My ex-husband's words resounded in my ears: "Why can't you put others before you?"

Maybe you can put others before yourself when you are happy with yourself and your relationship with your spouse and your children. But if none of these relationships are working, then that is a tremendous ask. Is the ultimate sacrifice to forget who you really are and become absorbed in your role, to be a mother, a father, a wife, a husband? This is where Michael was, uncomfortable in his skin, ready to shed it, and perhaps in a way that I wasn't entirely prepared for. I was fully aware of the role I was playing now in unleashing his soul. Being the great believer in destiny and providence, I felt the greater forces of the Universe at play here. I knew that I could be the catalyst that turned his life around, but I was at that moment completely unaware of the torrent of passion that was about to be released, not to mention the extraordinary pain of separation that we would both endure.

We began making our way back to the car, through the cobbled streets, holding hands and stopping every now and then to steal a kiss. We were so absorbed by each other and with the beauty of the moments that we became totally and utterly lost in the back streets of the city. I didn't mind. I hoped to be lost, wandering the streets of Bordeaux with him every day of my life, just so that we could steal some more time together. It was actually liberating, lost in the moment and being totally despairing to all reason. I didn't care what happened next, and gave in to spontaneity and what life was offering me right there and then.

That evening, after we managed to find our way back to

Place du Parlement, we drove home to the guest house at Le Bouscat. We sat in silence, his hand on mine the whole way, another impressive driving feat: one-handed on French roads! Eventually, the gates to our beautiful guest house opened. And it was like coming home.

Ever the gentleman, Michael insisted on opening my door. As I alighted from the car, he took my hand and we walked in silence into the house and up the stairs. He lead me directly to my bedroom. Not a word had been spoken since we got into the car and drove back; enough had been said.

"Forget about responsibility, Michael," I now said to him, "about trying to make everyone else happy."

We made love that night and neither of us felt any shame for breaking all the rules. But he was very quiet afterwards. He seemed withdrawn into his own world. Sensing his confusion, I simply stroked his head and whispered in his ear, "Don't worry it will all be OK. Have faith."

***

The following day I caught a cab to Vinexpo and began my perusal of wine labels and products, interspersed with frequent trips past his stand that were accompanied by longing glances and schoolgirl/schoolboy grins.

Michael had prior commitments that evening, but he came to my room upon his return from dinner. As I lay in bed waiting for the sound of his car and the anticipation of sneaking to him, I pondered again the predicament I felt was unfolding. The thought lasted for all of one millisecond, and promptly banished to the lost baggage department.

I could hear the rain outside and Michael had become

Sacrifice

absolutely soaked running from the car to the house. After one evening of lovemaking together I could not believe the ease we felt in each other's company. He slipped his clothes off and got under the sheets alongside my nakedness. We began cuddling as if we'd been together for years. I had not experienced this naturalness for a very, very long time and was quite swept away. I was powerless to control *it*... and felt wonderful!

The next morning I chose to spend walking and taking in Le Bouscat. There was a beautiful park I wanted to explore and photograph. I think I had found my real reason for attending Vinexpo, and it wasn't business. The day was grey and overcast, and muggy; too warm for a coat, so I took an umbrella. The following is an extract from a diary I kept of the holiday. It was a diary kept as a reminder of events.

> *'A slightly peculiar thing happened as I was walking down the street. Passing by a shop, which had a loud speaker blaring music onto the sidewalk, I was struck by the words of a song. It captured me. I had to stop and listen because it moved something inside me. I think it might have been the key to the massive padlock and chain that had been imprisoning my heart. I stood there under the umbrella listening to Elton John singing Sacrifice and cried. The tears flowed freely. I didn't want to analyze anything or ask myself "Why?" I think I cried for Michael, too.'*

I suddenly realized that I was going to miss him terribly after Vinexpo ended and we went back to our own lives. I felt confused about a lot of things, the tyranny of distance being the main one, and where Michael was at in respect to his personal circumstances. One thing I was sure of: I was falling in love, there was nothing I could do to stop it, and it felt so damned good.

***

That evening we joined a party of colleagues from the Australian and London wine trades at a jazz club. The restaurant was built during the 1920s and absolutely nothing had been altered. The walls were plastered with photographs of famous musicians in the haphazard way only the French can employ successfully. Anarchy was the design aesthetic. The furniture was in dire need of attention. I loved the fact that it was so old, so authentic, and that it offered such a contrast to Australia's trendy new café scene. We had to be very cautious that evening, as I was respectful of Michael's married status, though it was hard to hide such powerful feelings. It felt good just being by his side.

The presence of Michael's professional acquaintances did not seem to bother him. We sat next to each other and shared a creme brulée, which was to become "our" signature dessert, and played footsies under the table with abandon. When I wanted to go to the ladies' room, I could not find my shoe. I quietly asked Michael if he knew where it was. He immediately sunk below the table, to everyone's surprise, and surfaced a little while later with my shoe.

"Found it!" he shouted with guilty glee, and the other guests roared with laughter. I was embarrassed and flattered at the same time, having him flirt so openly and carelessly with me.

This was the night of the Fête de la Musique, held annually in Bordeaux during June. The streets were packed and the

Sacrifice

atmosphere was quite electric. However, we just wanted to go home to the lovely house in Le Bouscat and make love.

The following day, Michael played truant from his stand at the wine show and we took off into the French countryside for lunch and a meander around the 15th century town of St. Émilon, with its terracotta roofs, cobbled streets and wine cellars. As we wandered and explored, I could feel myself being drawn deeper into him. Just standing next to him gave me the most wonderful feeling of tranquility. I held back from telling him any of this; I was still afraid of the complications it would bring, fully believing that I was having one of those *'what happens on tour stays on tour experiences.'* He was married, and he was a client!

That evening, our last in Le Bouscat, we were left alone. Marcel had returned to Germany and the owners of the house were out to dinner. We had the whole joint to ourselves. I'm not sure what it is about being in love, but it sometimes feels like a childlike madness, an adolescent feeling of creating mischief and being able to get away with it. We talked and laughed about how we'd be able to make love all over the house, even in Madamé and Monsieur's bedroom (which was a disturbing thought really). We became intoxicated by the fact we were *'playing house,'* in someone else's home. It felt delirious and just slightly deranged.

We dashed down to the deli to collect our supper as we had done on the first evening, buying a magnificent array of small quiches, paté, cheeses and exquisite French things I'd never seen before. It was there on the verandah, on our last evening in the beautiful house in Le Bouscat, Bordeaux, that Michael declared his love for me. As badly as I wanted to say the same thing back to him, I innocently replied, "Oh boy, we are in trouble aren't we?"

"Yes, we are," he replied with a cheeky smile.

I told him of my experience the previous day, and how I felt when I'd heard Sacrifice blasting into the street. He simply took me by the hand and led me to his car, telling me that he had an even better rendition of the song. He turned on the ignition, inserted a tape and Sinead O'Connor began singing. Her voice soft and soulful, accompanied only by a piano, was a beautiful and stirring rendition. We listened. We did not touch or kiss or talk, for nothing could improve on the stillness of our souls harmonizing with the words that rang so true.

***

Love awakens many senses, and one that appeared heightened that week was taste. So much that we did involved fine food and wine. So to fuel our journey north towards England, we stocked the car with baguettes, brie, chocolate, strawberries, and mineral water; just a few essentials of life. That was an eventful little trip. On the way to the deli, a Frenchman backed into Michael's car, smashing its front left parking light. It wasn't serious, and the Frenchman was apologetic. A year later, he still had not yet repaired it, because it reminded him of that wonderful week in Bordeaux.

We were headed for Versailles, where we would spend a night before embarking on the hovercraft at Calais across the English Channel. Even though my travel plans were toward Italy, I had decided to at least accompany Michael back to England, if only to draw out our last few moments together. I had a girlfriend in London with whom I could stay.

On the way, we found a field of tall grass in the countryside surrounded by poplars to have our simple lunch of bread and brie and dashboard-warmed strawberries. Our joy seemed never

Sacrifice

ending, sitting on the car rug together in the tall grass, eating our simple lunch. We knew this was our last full day together, and the beauty of the moments lingered as the hours slowly unfolded.

We were aware that our time was now limited and were therefore conscious of the need to cherish every moment. It was an entire day's drive to Versailles, and I was not look-ing forward to so many hours in a car. Having dressed that morning in a transparent white cotton shirt, and my favorite lacey bra, which was both sexy and damned uncomfortable, I deliberated on my somewhat vain choice of attire for a car journey; suffer or take the stupid thing off! With comfort being paramount I decided it had to go. Using the esoteric magic technique known only to females (no male I have ever met has been able to comprehend it)—the through-the-armhole-elbow-gymnastic-routine—I eased it off and out from under my shirt. I thought I'd spice things up a little by handing it across to Michael. He kept his eyes on the road, but the look on his face suggested that indeed he did not object to the game at hand. He hung the bra from the rearview mirror, where it waived gently, both a trophy and a personal tribute to freedom.

We approached an accident and the traffic trickled to an almost standstill. As we drove by at a mere 15 kms per hour, it seemed all the attention became focused on the car with English number plates. I remember clearly the astonished and amused looks on the faces of the Gendarmerie as they peered in at me in my see-through blouse, bra hanging brazenly in the front window from the mirror! We felt like a couple of naughty little children on a joy ride, speeding through the countryside (for which he copped a hefty fine), playing loud music, feeding each other soft chocolate, and making a great mess.

I hate to think how we must have looked checking into the

hotel, but I know we had great big grins on our faces because we had agreed to see how quickly we could make love, when we got there. Then our record would be set for us to beat, when the occasion for quick sex arose. The clothes were coming off before we hit the room and once there got straight into some hot, sweaty, very quick, hilarious sex. I loved his antics, his ideas and the way he made me laugh constantly. He made me feel like a child again, but he also made me feel like the most precious woman on earth. If I was unleashing his soul, then he was leading mine into uncharted territory and I did not mind one bit.

***

Versailles was the finale to our week of magic, love and discovery. I was going to miss him terribly, for the next part of my travel agenda entailed a week in Taormina on the island of Sicily—alone again.

On the final day we headed for Calais and the English Channel. We reached Calais around midday and waited for the hovercraft to arrive, swallow us up and deposit us on England's shores at Dover. The twenty minute ride was simply not long enough. I wanted it to last all day, sitting there next to him, gin and tonics in hand, which went everywhere but in our mouths, kissing every two minutes like love sick teenagers, and touching each other fondly.

Time was eroding; we'd been tipping the hourglass back into each other, feeding the softly falling minutes into our memory, etching them as permanent and highly detailed fossils. An affirmation that our brilliant time together was coming to a close. When we arrived at Dover he turned to me, but before he said a word I had the uncanny feeling I already knew what he was

Sacrifice

going to say: "Welcome to my country".

The journey up to London was a stark contrast to the rest of the week. Landing on English soil and the sombre grey skies had dampened our spirits considerably and a gulf developed the closer we got to London. We were both saddened by the knowledge that we were soon to part and spent the entire trip in almost total silence. Michael was dropped me off at a girlfriend's place in London where I would be staying for a couple of days. He found it easily enough, though he also found a way of delaying time a little more by very kindly taking me on a condensed tour of London's tourist attractions: Buckingham Palace, the Tower of London, Westminster Abbey, St. Paul's Cathedral. But the time had come for us to part, so we agreed to meet again on Monday evening before I departed for Taormina, Italy. He wanted phone numbers of hotels, my home phone number in Australia, my work phone number in Australia, my girlfriends number, my parents phone number in New Zealand, stating that he did not want to lose me or let me slip away somehow and not be able to find me again. His words were very touching. I stood and watched him drive away and remained there well after he was gone.

"So," my friend said, "who is he and what's been happening? The electricity between you two was amazing!"

To think we were trying to be sedate and secretive! He phoned twice before he arrived home, which was a bit of a dead give away I guess. The second time was as he waited in his street ready to pull into his driveway and his real life again, and everything that would encompass.

He sent a card, which I received before our Monday rendezvous. It read: "Thank you for the most wonderful week of my life, Michael."

***

So this was what it felt like to go on a date. I had not felt like this for nearly twenty years. I'd been out with a few men since my divorce but none really interested me or compared with this wonderful feeling of anticipation. I literally could not wait to see his face again.

Michael took me to a restaurant called Ransoms Dock on the River Thames. It was a lovely evening during which he confided many things. One thing he touched on was the desire he'd had all his adult life to love a woman, to be one of those couples that walked hand in hand, or lay on top of each other in parks. How envious he had been of *those couples* and how much he had wanted to have that too. I don't think it is such a terribly obscure thing to want really. A mate to love. How basic and fundamentally human.

He had been holding my hand and as he moved it up towards my face he brushed my breasts and said, "It's nice, isn't it?"

I responded, "Yes, it is Michael, it's brilliant."

After we'd made love that evening, he went home to his wife and I prepared for my five day trip to Taormina. We agreed to meet again in a week's time when I returned from Italy, and before heading back to Australia, when my journey would be complete.

Well, that's what I thought. But in fact it had just begun.

***

For the final part of my European journey, I had searched for the most romantically inspired place in Europe and decided upon the township of Taormina on the island of Sicily. Why I chose this town, in hindsight, I don't know. It was an unlikely choice of place to meet someone or to find love, but it had been part of my

Sacrifice

plan, to escape my previous life and explore new countries. The fact that I'd chosen these romantic destin-ations was evidence of my need at the time, and was apparent in all that I was doing. I had cleaned up my backyard. All the weeds were gone. Now I wanted my life to blossom, to fully bloom with the intensity of a sunflower: Let the light in, I'm ready to grow!

I very nearly missed my flight to Sicily. Michael had ad-vised me to get the fast train out to Gatwick airport as a cab fare would have been horrendous. However, the train was not nearly fast enough and then, not being accustomed to such large airports, I got quite lost, agitated and disoriented as it became dangerously close to departure time. Once I'd checked in, airport staff called ahead to the aircraft. A mad sprint through three terminals and a monorail ride later I fin-ally boarded the plane, slumped into my seat and took a deep breath.

As I closed my eyes, I heard something very familiar. I initially thought it must have been my imagination. There was music. Sacrifice was playing on the plane's sound system. I closed my eyes and thought of Michael.

Although the bus broke down on the way from Catania airport, it wasn't long after my delayed arrival at the hotel in Taormina, having settled in by the pool, gin and tonic in hand, that the pool attendant came over to me with a phone, saying, "Excusa me senorina, phone!"

It was Michael, calling to say hello, wanting to feel me near and to say that he wished he was here with me too. He called every day without fail. From the moment I left France, I felt his presence ever with me. I fantasized of coming here again one day with him, for I held him so near in my heart and in my thoughts.

Taormina was delightful and more than I had anticipated. The shops were small and design-oriented, which attracted mainly wealthy Germans and French. The ambience attracted honeymooners and lovers. I made no friends because there were no English-speaking people and no singles to be found. However, a lot of very friendly Italian men followed and pestered me to the point where I had to get rude to be rid of them. I felt quite self-contained, happy to meander around on my own and write letters to Michael. The only part I found difficult was going to dinner and eating alone. The food was superb but I hated every minute of the dining experience.

***

Perhaps the Spanish island of Ibiza would have been a surer bet in finding love, or at least some great sex. But that was not my style, *the creative* in me inspired by beauty was drawn to the images in the brochures of endlessly winding medieval streets and tiny passages, cascading geraniums from balconied terraces, intimate restaurants, cafés, and gelateria.

Some of these intriguing places had secluded gardens hidden behind stone walls, others were set on terraces overlooking the coast, but all beckoned like good food to satisfy my soul's yearning for love and romance. Just as in Paris, I was happy to lose myself in the ambience, walking endlessly, soaking up the fascinating archeological monuments and beautiful homes. If romance can be measured in ambience, then I was totally loved up by Taormina.

I was enjoying myself immensely in this beautiful town, and with the freedom of no time pressures or other commitments I became curious to know more about the origins of Taormina. So I began to delve a little into its history.

I was not alone in my romantic inspiration, as it turned out.

Sacrifice

It was here that self-exiled *D.H. Lawrence* was inspired to write L*ady Chatterley's Lover,* one of the most passionate and erotic love stories of its era. Taormina also became a magnet during the nineteenth century for the European aristocracy and the artistic elite. Wilhelm Von Gloeden also lived in Taormina. His photography consisted mainly of frontal photographs of male nudes, which perhaps explains the attraction for gay men (mind you I have always found gay men to have impeccable taste). Taormina became known during this time as a Sicilian Monte Carlo, without the casino or royal family.

Taormina's earlier popularity, as history reveals, also led to civilizations who, rather than visit for a day or a week, would just invade the place and stay. In its early days, Taormina was a prime destination as far as military takeovers went.

It was originally settled by Greeks around 395 B.C. and came under the rule of the despot and tyrant Dionysius of Syracuse. Then named Tauromenion, it figured prominently in the regional politics of the next two centuries. The city surrendered to the Romans in 212 B.C. and became a Roman colony, a holiday resort for consuls and patricians who built many luxurious villas in this area, a *'cow to be milked'* for the Roman Empire. The Romans demanded heavier and heavier taxes from the city, and thus halted the economic development of the territory. Tauromenium flourished in the time of Julius Caesar, but by the fall of the Roman Empire (476 A.D.) the Byzantines had settled in. They were followed by a period of inhabitation of both Muslims and Christians who alternated in ruling the city until 962 A.D., when the Arabs finally mastered control and renamed it Almoezia.

In 1078 A.D. it was returned to Christian rule and given back its original name, Tauromenium. After the Christians, the Swabians arrived, followed by the French, and then the Swarbs again. After almost a century of conflict, Sicily passed into the hands of the Spanish and Palazzo Corvaja in Taormina became the seat of the Sicilian Parliament. There was a period of stability that lasted for several centuries, despite the heavy taxation imposed by the Spanish.

From 1713 onwards, Sicily fell under the rule of the Austrians and then back under the Spanish once more. Spanish dominion lasted until 1860 when the battleship Thousand reached Taormina under the leadership of Nino Bixio, an Italian soldier and politician, who fought for the Italian Unification. Which is how Sicily came to be under Italian rule today.

One thing was for sure, in the 21st century tourists now ruled supreme, and for good reason. Taormina was steeped in history and it wears its past beautifully. The Greek amphitheater built during the first period of reign still presented regular opera performances throughout the summer months, and the architecture from subsequent cultures created an eclectic and thoroughly interesting mix of historical interest.

After my days of sightseeing and cultural immersion, I would communicate with Michael in the evening writing letters:

Sacrifice

Thursday 27th June 1995
Dearest Michael,

Taormina is beautiful. Everything I pictured in my mind's eye has been fulfilled. I am deeply aware of my need to share it with someone. The only way I shall be able to enjoy this sojourn is by sharing it with you. Therefore you shall be getting the full account of my week here, the trivial and the touching. To imagine you here with me; so if I can detail my days to you by writing it all down, this is my way of saying thank you. I know you have been thinking of me every waking second, as I have of you too.

That first day we spent together (just last Sunday), I learnt so much about you, and by Thursday when we spent almost a full day together... well, I don't really know what I'm trying to say in this sentence, perhaps, "I love you." I think I knew it on Sunday, definitely by Thursday.

After dinner tonight, I headed out for a stroll and came across the elegant botanic gardens perched high on a ledge over the sea. It had been the private garden of an English noblewoman, Florence Trevelyan, and was bequeathed between

1890 and 1899 to the city of Taormina upon her death. The holiday month of August provides free evening performances for tourists. We are entertained by string quartets, puppet shows, and opera. I watched a puppet show this evening. The puppets are very appealing for their appearance and size, about three feet high, and very elaborately dressed. Even though it was in very passionate Italian, I could still understand the main play. All the couples wrapped around each other made me feel slightly sad and melancholy however.

I walked a lot that night through the tiny streets, which provide for pedestrian and motorcycle traffic only, observing all the outdoor cafes filled with tourists and locals and lovers everywhere! At one point I stopped to soak in a strumming singing minstrel who was wandering around serenading all the lovers. He had a lovely voice and of course the melody was romantic and the alley he was cruising was steep with very wide steps, upon which there were outdoor table settings crowded with customers. I stood at the bottom and just listened, looked and loved what I was feeling. It didn't matter that you weren't there, I felt you anyway.

On the way back to the hotel I was harassed by a dude who first wanted to take me to a disco, then to his place for dinner, and how about the beach tomorrow? He even tried "Ah, of course," my hotel! I was also followed by another man for quite some distance. I didn't like that one bit, but I seemed to

Sacrifice

lose him by stepping up my pace and I soon found myself at a cable car that went down the hillside to the beach. I thought that an evening stroll along the beach would be very soothing. I know what you are thinking...Sicily, Mafioso, yes probably a crazy idea especially after being followed like that. Sometimes I think I need protecting from myself!

It was around 11 p.m. and totally deserted anyway, which I liked (nothing worse than having other people around when you are on your own!) I sat on a deck chair and just basked in the moonlight, and closed my eyes. I could hear music from a club on the beach. It sounded familiar, and as I strained to make out the words I realized it was Sacrifice being sung in Italian.

The tears began again, but they were tears of joy found in the comfort of love and knowing, and I felt instantly warm and happy.

June 28th 1995
Time to hit the shops. A major attraction here in Taormina are the open-air markets held every Thursday morning. I happened across a stall with the most gorgeous Italian sarongs, with equally gorgeous Italian boys who were vying for my attention to the point I could not resist their taunts to "try it on."

So there I was, being wrapped and tied in various sarongs of alternate style and fabric over my shorts. Every fitting was personal—THEY had to wrap it and tie it onto me (they took turns in doing so). It was so much fun, I don't know how these guys get away with it really—only in Italy I guess. It was like flirting with a lot of consensual body contact. I found it quite confronting at first until I told myself, "ah, go on enjoy yourself," and before you knew it we were (all 3 of us) tying me up in knots! I only bargained 5,000 Lire off the price. I thought afterwards that they should have paid me for the fun they had.

Then on to buy a bikini, and again the same scenario—a man to help fit me with the correct size. It was quite an experience I can tell you! The clothes and swimwear in these tiny little shops are extraordinarily exquisite. The Italians have such a great sense of style and attention to detail, making the shopping excursion such a delight and something I have not experienced before. I just love meandering through these cobbled streets, which unravel surprises around every corner. Across from the bikini shop I purchased drinks for my room, and the big mamma at the counter asked if I would like a sandwich for lunch. How could I resist? I tell you, it was the simplest yet tastiest meal I'd had in a long while, a simple crusty roll with no butter, just ham and soft cheese, but the freshness—bellissimo!

I sat in the botanic gardens and shared my sandwich with a family of cats. The cats scavenge for food to survive in competition with the pigeons; it was quite amusing to watch this odd picture. I was enjoying all this on my own until some little

Sacrifice

Casanova came and ruined it all. No explanation needed!

The afternoon was spent by the pool, reading, dipping, sleeping, I'm now onto my second G&T (in my room) and the travel agency has just delivered a bottle of wine as compensation for the bus breakdown on the way here from the airport. I think it may be one of those nights! Perhaps after three G&Ts I may have the courage to ask someone if I could join them for dinner. We're dining on the terrace tonight, thank god. So, here I am with my partner — the trustworthy pad and pen — excuse the scrawl as I converse with you at 100 mph. I try to keep up with my thoughts, and they are racing right now. I'm sure any of those bored stoic couples would relish my company. I'd annoy the wife at the very least and turn the husband on at the very most, and probably be the focal point of their week.

Please, please, please don't let us ever get like that. Mediocrity destroyed my marriage, the blandness, the expectancy, normalcy, the boredom of it all. I'm afraid of all that, yet I still believe in it (marriage) so much, perhaps my expectations are unrealistic. I can't believe though how much I am enjoying just writing to you. I know of a saying, I don't know who said it, maybe I did, "That through a woman a man finds his soul, and through a man, the woman finds the desire to express herself."

You make me feel like a woman. I am so aware of it when I am with you and without you and that is quite frightening and beautiful all at once. Are we so individual in our persona yet so incomplete in our existence to feel this need to 'belong' with someone?

I wrote pages and pages of ramblings to you, which I tore up in the morning. Don't worry, I don't think you would have understood any of it, I didn't!

June 29th 1995
Considering the state of my head, I think I did admirably rising at 7 a.m. I had such a full day planned, and wasn't going to let a hangover ruin it. I felt like passing out in several shops and nearly vomited into the lions' pit at the amphitheater, but my survival instincts won out in the end and I came right at about midday. Going to the amphitheater early was a wise choice as there were next to no tourists. By the time I left, they were climbing all over the place and would have seriously ruined my photography session.

I had the roll of film developed from our week in Bordeaux. There were lots of you, of us; it was so good to see that it was not an illusion—because it felt like a dream. I lined them up on the bed and all the memories came flooding back, and they made me glow. I particularly like the one of us on the verandah, and am making a mental note to take as many of us as I possibly can when I return to London. I will need them to sustain me over the coming months without you. What a horrifying thought Michael, to only look at you. Not that you

Sacrifice

are horrific to look at — you know what I mean!

I was just about to embark on a walk to the beach when a massive cloud bucketed its load onto Taormina. It was quite welcome actually as the days have been hot and sticky.

June 30th 1995
Today I decided to do a tour, the most obvious one that most tourists visiting Sicily do, Mt. Etna. What can I say about tours apart from the fact I don't think I will ever embark upon a bus tour again. We went, we saw, we climbed it: I never want to do it again! I have decided that being a tourist 'en masse' is an extremely humiliating experience and I won't be hurrying back to the bus depot to be herded on the bus like sheep and solicited for souvenirs that would win the tackiest souvenir prize in any competition, hands down!

The mere thought of another evening in the 20 foot-high-ceiling dining room with the leering waiters was too much for any further contemplation, so I headed into town in search of a cozy café for a plate of simple pasta and a glass of red. There are so many restaurants, all with red-checked tablecloths, candle in glass and grapevine entwined verandahs overhead.

A group of English speaking people soon arrived. Some were American, some with French accents. I wondered if they were all on vacation together or had just met at the hotel and become friends; anyway I wanted to join them so badly and be a part of their conversation.

If I had not met you, Michael, Taormina would have been a very lonely experience. It is a place full of couples, both heterosexual and homosexual (lots of them), a destination for lovers and honeymooners. I was lonely, but this would have been compounded had I not met you. The romance and ambience of Taormina's cobbled streets, intimate restaurants, and quaint shops has only fueled the romance already stirring in my heart. I have carried you everywhere I have been in Taormina.

After dinner I headed for the Botanic Gardens once more. Tonight I listened to a string quartet. It was very beautiful, civilized and so very Italian. My last night in Taormina, I stayed and soaked in the lights from the bay and the township on the cliffs, and thought how very fortunate I was to have experienced such a wonderful place, and to have met you. Independent as I am, I do yearn for the completeness of having a man, a very special man who complements my being. I know that there is a huge 'test' of our love before us. I am prepared for that test, because I, of all people, probably need that test.

What I am trying to say Michael, is that after only one week, my feelings for you are intense, and that only the separation and tyranny of distance will truly reveal the truth. For at the moment, I am living the life I imagined I could have and feel that I am subconsciously making it all happen, too.

Sacrifice

I came from the other side of the world searching for romance. I chose destinations that I thought this might happen: Paris, London, and Taormina, but I found it with you in Bordeaux.

Also, for you the distance and separation will indicate clearly what is important in your life, and how you want to deal with the predicament we have found ourselves in. I do have great faith in destiny and that whatever is to be, will be. And that sometimes you need to actively take part in your own destiny.

On the way back to the hotel after dinner I collected a 'souvenir' when a motorcyclist without a light struck me head on! I made such a hullabaloo about it in English, but in true Italian style, with great passion, hand gestures and lots of 'F' words. Nobody came to my rescue, or said sorry. They could see I was coping in true Italian style, I guess. And so now I have two very bruised legs for you to see.

I shall no doubt see you in London very soon and probably before this letter arrives! Thank you for a week filled with memories. You were here in my heart the whole time.

Barbara

I returned to England to stay with another friend for the weekend. Because he was a male friend and had very kindly given up his bedroom for me, as had my girlfriend previously, I would not have felt right about making it with Michael there. Why I felt okay about making love in my girlfriend's bed, but not my male friend's bed, I don't really know.

Therefore I had suggested to Michael that he find some hotel accommodation for us on my last night in England, for privacy. He picked me up on Sunday from my friend's house and we spent the day at the Henley Boat Regatta, the annual two-day rowing event between Oxford and Cambridge University held on the Thames. Michael packed a picnic, which we had amongst the cars where there was more privacy than on the banks of the river with the throngs of other picnickers. Michael had never done 'Henley' in this fashion before, steering well away from tents or spots which may have involved bumping into someone he knew. It was a Henley he had not seen before, the hot dog stands, candyfloss machines, and T-shirt tents (which had every conceivable crass saying available under the sun). When he saw bungee jumping from a crane, he exclaimed, "Christ, what has the British Empire come to?" I could sense his immense dissatisfaction with England, but I laughed at his comment and was quite amused by it all.

The little hotel I had asked him to book turned out to be a fine old English manor called Oakley Court, situated right on the Thames, not far from Windsor. It was more than comfortable in its opulence, and very romantic. Michael said he'd always wanted to stay here and now he had the perfect occasion.

As we sat in the hotel room opposite each other, the realization of paths to follow, where they may lead, and the logistical nightmare of distance, all loomed before us. I would go back to my

Sacrifice

newly built townhouse in Adelaide, with my friends, my sons, my twenty-four year-old boyfriend (who had quite rapidly become a very distant memory), the sun, and the convivial lifestyle I led. Michael would remain in England facing a marriage crisis, family opinions and a lifestyle he abhorred in many respects. I did not envy him one bit. As we sat there wondering what would evolve from this romantic liaison, he looked up at me and beckoned for me to come to him. I went to him and just curled up in his arms. His huge frame enveloping my petite body made me feel so helpless and childlike. I was astounded at the array of feelings I had with this man. He could make me feel vulnerable and yet he also gave me such a great sense of my own feminine power.

Our love was always adaptable to the moment. Unlike our playful love making at Versailles, we weren't eager for each other's bodies, for the sadness of our separation was all too real.

I could have sat on his knee curled up and comforted, forever. I'll never forget the poignancy of these precious moments that seemed to etch a deep groove into my memory. He said he could not stay with me, though I think he was incredibly tempted to. Later, he told me he very nearly just turned around and drove back after leaving.

I lay there for hours on the massive king-size bed after he had gone, reliving the events of the past two weeks, knowing that our meeting had changed both our lives irrevocably. What do I do? What could I do? Nothing. It was Michael's life that needed a serious overhaul and only time would be the telling factor of his sincerity and determination to change his life—and only if he really wanted to.

June 29th 1995
My dearest Barbara,

It's a glorious summer day. The sky is a pale blue, the grass and the trees a marvelous shade of green, there are flowers aplenty adding the warmth of color and variety. I have come up to my golf club for peace, contemplation, and a stunning view. The club is set in the grounds of Brocket Hall, a stately home in Welwyn, some ten minutes away from home and the office. From where I am sitting I can see the hall, built in 1765, the old oak tree under which Queen Elizabeth the first sat when she was under house arrest, the beautiful arched bridge over the lake, and of course, the odd golfer! It is truly a magical place, especially in the warmth of a summer's day. The only thing that would improve the situation is if I could turn and gaze into your shining eyes, reach out to hold your hand, and to share the pleasure of the moment, one day perhaps.

The plan is to give you this letter on Monday. I wonder if I can wait that long! If so, then you will probably be reading this as you sit on the plane

Sacrifice

facing the long and tedious journey to the Orient. The sad thing is, the longer you read this, the further away from me (geographically only) you become. The great silver bird in the sky is carrying you off to your far distant nest after your all-too-brief visit to the great northern hemisphere! And what a trip it was—there has hardly been a waking moment during which I haven't relived some of the great things that have happened to us, from the time I scaled the stairs at the Timotel in Paris that gray Sunday morning. As I turned the corner into the lounge and saw you sitting quietly and patiently there, something, I'm not sure what, stirred. I was genuinely excited to see you, really relishing the prospect of driving south with you, getting to know you. Somehow, I just felt so at ease with you. The more we talked, the more I glanced at you, the more I knew that there could be a bond of some sort between us.

I know we have talked of many things in the short time since we met, but I hope you will excuse me repeating the fact that you have become such a very special part of my life. I thought I knew myself, knew my heart, but only you have been able to teach me so much. How I admire you, and what you have done. How I envy your assuredness, your calm, your sereneness. Sometimes, many times these days, I have felt my emotions locked up, so much so that at times I genuinely forget they are there at all. You have come along like some latter day savior on an emotional white charger to free my feelings and to allow them to gaze on green and fertile pastures, instead of being trapped in the gray dungeon of a marriage without love. I knew one day I could express and feel the thoughts and emotions I wanted to express and feel. All those thoughts and emotions are locked into your direction with the unfailing accuracy of a scud missile with laser guided sights.

This is a long winded way of saying, 'Barbara, I love you!' I love you in a way I have not experienced in all my married life, if ever, and with an intensity that is almost frightening. I know that fate brought us together, that fate is putting distance and time between us, but fate will bring us together again, of that I feel so sure. I'm not sure I know when or how or where, but I have faith that our love and our happiness are destined to be shared. You have come to mean so much to me, and I positively shiver with excitement whenever you reciprocate those feelings. As you know, I am insecure in so many ways. I guess I always have been (product of the English public school system!), and to hear you say some of the lovely things you say about me makes me feel so special. I can hardly believe it. I have missed that for so long, how I craved it, but from the right person, that's the important part.

The sun is getting a little lower, the shadows are lengthening, and the breeze is like the delicate touch of your fingers on my arm, neck, and head. Perhaps it's time to end the letter—actually I may just call you, just to hear your lovely voice and to

Sacrifice

help me visualize your beauty—as if I need help in seeing you in my mind.

I could write all day long, a veritable epistle to you, there is so much I want to say. I seem to have erred on the poetic/romantic side, perhaps another letter will have a raunchier tone! (Now that's got me thinking about your delicious body.) Of all the memories I have of our togetherness, the times we had when our bodies met with love, tenderness and passion were the most memorable. A case of 'unfinished business'.

> A bientot, my dearest friend.
> This comes with all my love,
> Michael

July 4th 1995
Dear Michael,

Things have started to go wrong, but considering it is the last leg of my trip I should not complain. I think part of the reason things have gone so smoothly for me was because I had been so very well cared for during my time with you.

The flight to Hong Kong was the worst I

have ever experienced, stuck between two Asian gentlemen, one who was profusely and continually spitting into his sick bag throughout the entire journey. Consequently I lost my appetite and have only been able to face coffee and chocolate.

Just sitting here writing to you is of great comfort to me, it's all I have wanted to do, and get into my own bed for much needed sleep. Considering I had eight hours between flights, I decided to catch a bus into Kowloon with the idea of taking a ferry ride onto the harbor. It was overcast, humid and very sticky. I found a bus into town and it chugged along in a traffic jam for about an hour. The motion just rocked me off to sleep after the long flight and I also had two whole seats to myself, pure luxury after cattle class! So I sat there in a dreary semi-comatose state, the apartments and grime not enthralling enough to keep my senses even fifty-percent tuned in. Consequently, when I got off the bus, I realized that someone had run off with my Nikon, which I had stupidly placed on the seat beside me. I was so upset, Michael, mainly because of the priceless shots inside. The camera is insured, so I made sure that I filed a police report upon my return to the airport.

So there I was, on the harbor front in Kowloon, wishing I were anywhere but here, trying to muster up the necessary enthusiasm to take a ferry ride. Which I did, but the crowds were annoying me, their chitter-chatter grating on my nerves; the calm and serenity of the past two weeks had imploded!

Sacrifice

Halfway across the harbor the sky opened up, for it seemed to have empathy for my predicament, and the view of Hong Kong was obliterated completely.

I am so tired, Michael. I hope I will sleep on the next leg of the journey. Both movies they played I'd seen, but one was a favorite, so I did not mind watching it again, Rob Roy. You were Rob Roy and I was Mary McGregor. There are some delicious love scenes in it. He reminded me of you too, tall and solid!

I have such fond memories of our last night together, and no one can steal those away from me. The reality of the distance between us brought me down somewhat from my cloud. I feel as though I am about to wake from the dream state and all will be as it was, albeit with an added dimension to my life. How strange it will be, to be in love and only express it by letters! Perhaps that is why this has happened, so that we can become better communicators than we were, to be honest and true with each other. For you, there had not been enough physical love, and on my part perhaps too much of the wrong sort.

Your letter was lovely (my scud missile) and thank you for the photo, (but I do prefer you in blue jeans and moccasins, and I know you do too).

Second leg of the trip, the check in clerk must have felt sorry for me after my outpouring of bad luck and has given me a complete row of four empty seats, pure bliss! Good night my darling,

Barbara

And so it was that I returned to Australia with a thud, thinking, I've just had the most wonderful holiday romance with a married man. It was sublime, and I must leave it at that.

I was content that I had experienced such joy within myself, and with another person, but the reality of the situation began to hit home.

Returning from the European summer and my whirlwind romance to Australia's mild winter was a contrast, but not as great as the contrast I felt within myself compared to when I had left only three weeks earlier. The boyfriend, twelve years my junior, eagerly awaiting my return, held little interest for me. He'd been so entertaining over the past couple of months and I'd come to accept that all I wanted or was going to get from him was sex. He was a fantastic lover and terribly inventive. But suddenly his antics, boyishness and sexual gymnastics bored me, and I now found him positively irritating.

So I said goodbye. Good fun that he was, I felt he'd make someone else a lot happier.

Sacrifice

July 9th 1995
My Darling Barbara,

How lovely it was to talk with you on Friday. I had been thinking of you so much since your flight back, and it was great to hear your soft, calm voice. It just gave me so much happiness and energy. I'd had a lousy few days, feeling rather depressed about life in general, and perhaps still torn between the reality of your departure, and the quite fantastic memories of our days together, and the love we now share. On Saturday it was a lovely warm and sunny day, and I decided I needed the solitude of the golf course! I didn't play all that well, but it was good to get some sun, good company, and the sort of light-hearted banter that seems to pervade the golf course. On the way home, I was thinking of you as I drove through the lanes bordered by fields of ripening wheat, near the spot I shall always remember, as it was from there I phoned you while you were in Taormina. Anyway, I suddenly had a premonition that your letter had arrived already, as you would not have been able to post it until Wednesday. This seemed hardly likely, but I was convinced, so called by the office, and almost feverishly went through the pile of mail. My heart literally leapt when I saw your distinctive handwriting! I was just so excited — stupid isn't it, just like when we were teenagers!

I couldn't wait to read it, and sat in the sun at home and just soaked up your 'presence.' I am so sorry that you had such a dreadful journey home. I had a horrible feeling that the flights were going to be unsavory, and that Hong Kong would be an anticlimax. It sounded awful, especially with your camera being stolen, too. I presume that the film had the photos of us at Oakley Court and Windsor? I was really looking forward to seeing them. However, I have so many images of you and of us so indelibly imprinted in my mind, that nothing can erase these, and I feed on them, as surely as man needs air to breathe. In fact, so very many times during the day, and night too, I recall times, places, jokes, conversations, images, looks, sounds, smells, feelings — passionate ones, loving ones, moments of joy, of utter peace, and above all, thankfulness for the destiny that brought us together.

When I am driving the car, I find myself resting my hand on your imaginary hand or leg in the passenger seat. I glance across at you and smile, and you smile back, just as you did on our long journeys to and from paradise. Often during the

Sacrifice

day, or when I am lying in bed, and I am thinking of you, I just suddenly smile. You have transformed my life, the way I think, the way I act, the way I feel. My horizons, aspirations, ambitions have all been touched by what I have begun to feel—and the important thing is, I love it!

When I sat down to write this letter, I thought I would try to make it as conversational as possible, full of stories and anecdotes and a description of what I have been up to over the last few days, but somehow all I seem to be able to do is express some of the emotions I am feeling. I hesitate. I am concerned about doing this. I feel I may overwhelm you by telling you of all my innermost feelings, and how my thoughts about you dominate my life.

I fear that you may feel swamped by this, especially as you are now back home, with memories of what might seem to be a glorious yet temporary flight into a different world. If I bare my soul and reveal all that swims in my mind at the moment, please forgive me. Yet I make little apology for it.

I am sitting at the kitchen table on Sunday evening. It is still very warm, humid even. It has been a hot day (around 30 Celsius) and I took my son to cricket coaching this morning, stopping off on the way back at a place of solace by a stream, and another wheat field, just to feel your presence, think of you, laugh with you, hold you close. I'm afraid it made me a trifle sad, I missed you so much. There was nobody about, and I pointed in what I thought was the general direction of Adelaide, and shouted at the top of my voice "Barbara, I love you! I want to be with you! I will be with you!"

Did you hear me? I seem to have my whole life in a different perspective these days. Nothing is as it was, as you know, my marriage is a fifteen-year disaster, and now the pain is so acute it cannot be ignored. I have come to terms completely with life without my wife, and I am at peace with that. I just haven't found the right way of discussing the best, most dignified way of giving us both the chance of rebuilding our lives, and for our children. I know it will be best for all four of us when the realization of the sham is fully exposed. I know the children will understand eventually. But my whole outlook on so many things has altered. I so dearly want change—I want my life to take on a completely new meaning. I have tasted the nectar of emotions that I quite genuinely have not felt for twenty years. I want to uproot, discard old soils, and find a new more fertile pasture in another land, one that I love, to be with the one that I love. You said that time and distance will test our feelings, that destiny does not push you where you don't want to go. You're the one to choose, and to find that level, ask for guidance, and trust you'll be led wherever you most need to go—to try it!

Dear Barbara, I am tired, and I've had a couple of glasses of Rutherglen Muscat. I think I have rambled awfully in this letter, and I'm beginning to feel melancholy. I don't want to be here, a pom!

Sacrifice

I want to be with you in Australia, across the great expanse of land and ocean, my darling, I send you all my love...

Michael

The teacher will open the door,
...but only you can go through it

Anon

CHAPTER 2

Two Separate Worlds

[AUSTRALIA - Adelaide - July - November / 1995]

Construction on my townhouse was completed soon after I arrived back in Adelaide. During the tumultuous years towards the end of the marriage, I had dreamed and visualized owning a place of my own. I particularity wanted to have my own bedroom rather than camping out in the spare room, which was where I preferred to sleep rather than by my husband's side in the marital bed. It had become too difficult to be in the same bed with someone I no longer loved, and just being beside him even in sleep felt like I was betraying myself. We were no longer physical with each other, so why bother sharing the same bed?

When my settlement came through, one of the first things I did was put a deposit on a home of my own, undecorated, so that I could personalize the spaces with fixtures of my own choosing. Here I was, settling into life as a single woman with a 'room of my own' at last. I reveled in my new pad, pottering away, decorating with the furniture we had divided between us. I had no need to exorcise the past through purchasing completely new household items. I had chosen most of them anyway, so was happy to work with what I had. I'd also become a bit of an expert at dismantling the house and reassembling it in a new way. We had worked on the mines throughout Australia and had counted twenty moves in the eighteen years of our time together, as the company sometimes sent us to places for a duration of only six months, and it was always lock stock and barrel. I had seen my home come out of the back of a truck in boxes far too many times to remember with any fondness. Being a single person also meant that I chose stability in my life, something I had also yearned for as I grew into myself and my new single life.

Michael, on the other hand, was preparing for his family's annual European summer holiday, where he intended to shed his skin and expose the truth he longed for.

July 20th 1995
My dearest Barbara,

I just had to start a letter to you. I hope I can finish it tomorrow and post before I head off to Italy. Today held so many good things in store for me. Firstly, it was a beautiful morning, clear blue sky, birds singing, warm sunshine, trees full of color, flowers offering their sweet scent. The day became actually bloody hot (32 Celsius) but I'm not complaining. I woke early, thinking of you as always (a great start to any day). I remember you in bed looking so serene—calm and kind. I could never tire of gazing at you, drinking in your presence and the attraction your body and soul holds for me.

Anyway, your letter was there to greet me at the office. Each letter that arrives thrills me more. I can't tell you how much they mean to me. I spoke to you on the telephone and we talked of seeing each other soon (time will pass quickly, I'm sure). We talked of Tuscany, God what a wonderful thought, possibly the most romantic place on earth (so I'm told), after Bordeaux of course! I've already started looking at holiday brochures and dreaming of being with you there. We have so much in common and that is something I yearn to exploit. I have lived such a lonely marriage, devoid of the sharing of moments, feelings, events, humor, whilst at the same time respecting individualism, independence and certain points of difference.

Your letter was so full of happiness about your situation, and that does give me hope and inspiration. I hope I am as strong and as lucky. I envy you, but you have made it happen and I really applaud you. I remember during our drive from Paris quite early on, I was talking about selfishness and I sensed I had touched a raw nerve, and I immediately felt guilty. Now I know the part that selfishness has to play in certain situations. We are born, I suppose, loving ourselves, as it were. We only learn later about others. We, as individuals have to be at one with ourselves in order to make others at one with us. It is perhaps easy to confuse these issues and I certainly have been guilty of that. Piously thinking that I was being so bloody unselfish and understanding when really I was at odds with what I wanted, and therefore spoilt all things and people around me. You have helped me understand all that, but I still so admire your courage, your conviction, and your self assurance.

I love your expression of "the harmony playing inside me" and the "very mellow rhythm carrying me along". The words caress me as effectively as any of your soft kisses and gentle touch. God, how I yearn for your kisses, that warm embrace, like the one at your window in Bordeaux, the kiss that sent me to heaven!

I do often wonder about destiny and how we can shape it, and how some things are meant to be. I think and dream of us being together and it just seems so right. Perhaps it's like one of your label concepts, the broad outline plan is there, and won't change, because it's such a good concept; it's just the detail that has to be filled in by stages. I don't yet know when, how or where, but I know, hope, dream, and yearn that we will be together to exploit our special relationship and build upon it so that more and more happiness, in different ways and by different degrees, can be achieved. I've never been so sure of something. I too have faith in love. I didn't, but that was because love was buried deep within me. You rolled away the stone and your light and warmth flooded in to bring me energy and positive thoughts and love in abundance for me to shower upon you. We could

Sacrifice

conquer the world together!
I've scribbled enough tonight, and its late.

Michael

July 22nd 1995
Dear Michael,

Again, so good to hear your voice. Incidentally you were the inaugural caller in my new home! Am sitting on la couch, this time with coffee table (trunk) for my cup of tea, listening to beautiful music and writing to you.

I have been so excited by the turn in the tide and feel a lot of my old self returning—the part of me I did not want to discard but felt I had in order to 'make things happen'. Isn't it strange how we can cut off the love to another human being in our life, but feel so wretched and unloved in the process? The detriment of cause and effect I guess. My role as a mother I did not necessarily want to forego but found I had to, temporarily at least. As a result the boys had always begrudgingly come to stay with me and only in times of necessity, which I have found incredibly sad. I had hoped that in time they would forgive me or at least understand why I had to leave.

When my older son called last night to ask if he could come over for the day AND stay the night, well I went into shock!

Perhaps they are finally starting to accept me for who I am without resentment for what I did. Or perhaps it was seeing his father come home at 9am. in the morning in a dinner suit?

So I lapped it up and made chocolate brownies and a favorite chicken dinner, because I still love being a mum, possibly even more so on my own without the negativity of our unhappiness bearing down on us all. Maybe the realization that we can all be happy as individuals is starting to hit home at last. With this re-awakening of my mothering role and you in my life, I am also feeling a certain 'return to love'.

You may be surprised at how little you feel or think of your children. I went through this, always questioning myself as to why I didn't 'feel anything'. Perhaps this is our natural emotional mechanism closing down in preparation for what lies ahead. Thankfully it does come back.

But to also see my ex-husband happy (obviously events have changed over this past week with the boys away skiing) and feeling good about himself and his future just made me feel so wonderful too. I want someone to love him, to make him feel good. There will always be love between us, but now it is more of a respectful love mixed with the

Sacrifice

memories of a past life we shared, the children we had together and of course all the good times.

I know the divorce is probably only a matter of months away now. How long I have waited for this and yet strangely I feel sad because I am finally letting go. Now I know that we can never hold on, nor should we and that loving is also about letting go.

I am so thankful that we had such a wonderful life together, well ten years of it anyway, as I can't say the last eight have been that fantastic. But I always want to remember him for all the good times we had, for there were many. Today he actually thanked me for instigating it all and admitted (reluctantly) that he had not been happy, either.

I don't envy your task ahead. What you are about to do will be the most difficult thing you will ever do in your whole life, that I can vouch for! But you are also starting a journey for yourself, and how fantastic and exciting is that? Hold positive thoughts close to your heart and have faith in yourself and everything will naturally sort itself out, you will see, let love guide you.'

Barbara

AMALFI ITALY

August 2nd 1995
Darling Barbara,

This stretch of coastline has got to be one of the most spectacular in the whole Mediterranean. The towns, villages, villas, homes, and hotels literally cling to the sheer rock faces that rise steeply from the clear, sparkling sea.
The coast road was constructed in the mid-1800s, though quite how they built it defies imagination. Clearly the builders had no thought to the width needed when two large air-conditioned coaches meet on a hairpin bend. Despite this, hundreds of coaches, thousands of cars and millions of little motorcycles race along the roads all blaring their horns nonstop and each missing each other and the overhanging rocks by millimeters. Add to all this an assortment of pedestrians who have to walk without pavements and you have a recipe for carnage. Although each and every vehicle had dents and scrapes practically from the first day out of the showroom, no-one seems in the slightest bit

Sacrifice

bothered.

How much there is here that I have wanted to share with you. The scenic beauty, the food and wine, the characters, the history, the romantic air, the warmth of the sun, the cool clear water, and of course the double bed. Instead, this is an empty holiday, one devoid of all meaning and any joy or happiness.

It got off to an awful start. The journey began with a 4am. wake up, and was actually fairly uneventful, except for the usual Italian cock-ups at Naples airport in the steaming midday sun. Once we got to the hotel we realized that four stars in the brochure was rated on a completely different star system than one could conceivably imagine. This place puts Faulty Towers up there with the Ritz. Though the staff are friendly, the whole place needs a massive face-lift. It is practically falling apart, and when like everywhere else, it is built on the side of a cliff, it is not very reassuring.

Last night we had a storm with quite high winds, and after the lights went out for the third time, I genuinely expected to wake up under a hundred tons of rubble at the bottom of the cliff! Anyway, the food is adequate (just) and at least we can have breakfast outside on the balcony. Our room has a good view over the bay, though it doesn't get the evening sun. There are 200 steps down to the water (a jetty, as there are very few beaches as such) and we have a salt water pool which is quite a decent size.

Of course, the main problem at first was the tension between us. On Saturday night it just seemed right to come straight out with what I thought we should do. To my surprise, she took it quite well, and we had a pretty good chat about how we could and should ensure that the separation was, and was seen to be, completely mutual, without blame on either side. There were tears, and anxiety about how she would cope, but the over riding feeling was actually one of relief, perhaps both of us wishing we had done this years ago.

The big question was, and still is, as I write this, how to tell the children? This task will be much, much more burdensome. We have decided on the coming weekend, giving us all another week to come to terms with everything. I have to say I am not relishing this at all. I know that in the long run they will be happier, and because of the absence of acrimony, the parenting can be done without trauma, I hope.

I still fear that they will find it hard to understand exactly why we have to do it. For me, despite my anxiety about the children, I feel totally at peace with my decision. I know that there was no real love and thus an empty lonely life. I also know the kind of emotion, feeling, love, and capacity to give and receive of which I am capable—meeting you has given me that—and I do not want to waste the opportunity.

There is so much to share, so much I haven't shared for so long, and I yearn to do just that. It

Sacrifice

seems ironic that you were in Taormina, and I now in Amalfi, each privately enjoying the splendor of the place, but each sad not to be sharing it physically with the other. What a waste!

Never mind, the future holds many, many happy shared scenes, moments, smells, experiences, and nights of love, romance and passion (plus the odd bout of lust thrown in for good measure). The place is secondary, but the partners are primary. Any place—from Adelaide to Amalfi, from London to Sydney, from Tuscany to Kangaroo Island, from the Whitsunday Islands to the wilds of Scotland—all are fine, so long as you are there with me. Any place can become our Bordeaux.

I am now sitting on the balcony in the warm night air, gazing over the dark sea with the lights of Amalfi in the distance, the lapping of the water below, the buzz of a hundred mosquitoes around me, and the flow of a gin and tonic ensuring the somewhat staccato flow of my pen.

Many times have I sat here thinking of you, wishing and willing to be beside you, to reach out and touch you, to caress you with thought word and deed (especially deed). The family are asleep—I am scheming the shaping of my destiny. Fearing the path I want to tread, but the trepidation is exciting and stimulating nonetheless.

I hope this letter survives the vagaries of the Italian postal system and you receive it sometime before Vesuvius erupts again. I long to get home to receive your letters. I do so love reading them.

> *As always with this letter comes all my love, my fondness and feelings for you are not even surpassed by the stunning beauty of this coastline. I can't wait to see you again.*
>
> *Michael*

There he was, in one of the most romantic places on earth, writing to me and betraying his wife in doing so. Then why did it feel so right, why did I not feel guilty? How could I do this to another woman, to a family? Where was my solidarity to the Sisterhood?

I had been there in her shoes as well, and knew that these situations in relationships are not one-sided. It's just a matter of which person is first to say, *"I've had enough, let's call it a day and move on."* It's much easier to stay than move on in many respects. After all, who wants to face the upheaval of selling the family home and splitting assets, not to mention the explanation to friends and family who had no idea just how untenable life had become? But that is all it is when it comes to the real end of relationship: property, furniture, cars, and maybe investments, are just glue keeping the seams together, while the stitching has all but frayed and disappeared.

Michael's penning of intimate thoughts only clarified his commitment to our future together. They clarified his love for me and that he was hell-bent on making it happen. The time was now.

***

Sacrifice

August 5th 1995
Darling Barbara,

How bitter and how sweet life can sometimes be. Yesterday brought such a mixture of pain and pleasure. It started with a warm sun, a lovely view and a telephone conversation to gladden any heart. Your warm, soft voice—seemingly so near, defying the miles between us. It's good to chat about daily lives and trivia as well as exchange expressions of deep feeling. It was indeed a great start to the day.

Later that day, whilst enjoying a spell on a hot and crowded beach, down at least 400 stone steps from the road, we decided to tell the children. It was going to be whilst out at sea when we hired a pedal boat, but the children were so excited, it just did not seem right.

Therefore at lunch in the café, I just leaned across and came right out with it: "Mummy and Daddy have decided to separate."

At first they laughed and thought I was joking, then suddenly both their faces dissolved into a look of abject despair, and tears welled up and *spilled uncontrollably. Barbara, I have never felt so wretched in my whole life. My throat hurt as I fought back the tears and as I tried to explain, without too much detail, some of the reasons why we had reached this decision and how they were not to blame.*

This is Italy after all, and the granny who ran the café suddenly came up to my daughter and tried to console the child even though she had no idea what the problem was. She covered her in hugs and kept patting her hair and saying soothing things in Italian! Interestingly, they composed themselves quite quickly, and bar a few questions about houses and pets, etc., they were really very understanding.

My wife, to her credit, was very good and reassured them time and again that it was a fully mutual decision, and all would be done to lesson the pain and difficulty. We actually spent a good afternoon with all of us very close and being especially 'nice' to each other.

However, in the 24 hours or so since there have been more tears and sudden uncomprehending emotion that have saddened me. My daughter is worried for me, how I will cope on my own, how lonely I will be etc. My emotions are curiously mixed. My overriding feeling is one of wanting what is best for them to be happy, especially when I see their sad eyes so full of the unknown, but I have absolutely no sense of regret. It's more relief, though I too am fearful of the future.

But I do see happiness ahead, for each of us, in

Sacrifice

time. I know it, I believe it, and I am relaxed deep down. I think they trust me, and now I trust myself. I am steeled in my resolve to find happiness with one I love and to have a life full of fulfillment, joy and meaning. But I will miss their closeness, and whilst I will always give them as much love as I can, perhaps I will regret that I could not give them that ultimate security of a neat family structure right through until they flee the nest. But then, life was never meant to be straight forward, was it? I must stay strong for them.

There is a moon tonight, its light playing on the calm waters below, joining the lights of the fishing boats, and the air is full of the sounds of local people enjoying a 'festival Saturday'. We had fireworks (in a typically haphazard Italian fashion) earlier, and now the sounds of Whitney Houston's - I Will Always Love You (how apt). I've not heard Sacrifice yet, but I hear it in my mind.

This and many other things remind me of you and that makes me happy. You have said that time and parting and the distance between us will test our feelings. Mine have felt like concrete filling the foundations of a grand and beautiful new building. There is more to come to complete the edifice. Like all great works of art, nothing can be rushed and detailed plans have to be followed. But with the right will, the right materials, the artistic flair and creativity, the end result will be something to behold! I long to be with you,

Michael

It was out, and he did it without reference to me, which I was so grateful for. It seemed evident that his wife was also relieved, so that wasn't so bad was it?

Yet I have to admit that I didn't feel fantastic about it. I knew I was the reason, the catalyst for him to make the break he had so wanted for too many years. It was a huge step for him; it all looked easy from here on, in theory.

This was the biggest obstacle, we both knew, so I tried to reassure him, but felt shallow in my efforts. I guess my moral compass was just a bit overloaded and stuck on south.

August 7th 1995
Dear Michael,

You sounded quite withdrawn on the telephone, but considering the circumstances I do understand. I bet you are not looking forward to breaking the news to everyone else either. Having been there myself, Michael, it's not that bad, really, people wont judge you when the decision is a mutual one and therefore amicable. You are on that road now, going down a new path, you are on your way. Probably got a couple of hundred miles to go, which will take you the best part of two years to do. But what's two years in comparison to fifteen, or the

Sacrifice

rest of your life? You should be feeling ecstatic! Maybe you are, deep down, but still feeling a lot of concern for everyone else's welfare. It sounds like the holiday was at least a good excuse for all this to happen. I know it takes a lot of courage, and I am proud of you.

Adelaide has been so wet, honestly I have never known it to rain so much. I have settled in amazingly well and love my new pad along with the singledom of having it all to myself. Is that a tad selfish? Well if it is, it's overdue!

I saw a movie on Friday night, a French film - Queen Margot. It was terribly blood thirsty yet strangely erotic, filled with gorgeous women and men and bodies everywhere (dead, mostly naked!). There was one scene where the Queen goes looking for a man for the night because she's hungry. She wears a mask over her eyes as a disguise and chooses this nimble young animal who screws her instantly up against a stone wall, and does this so well he later becomes her full time lover (surprise, surprise!).

In one scene he says to her, "I recognized you even though you were wearing a mask." It made me think of how you recognized me in the Timotel Hotel in Paris. Is this what you meant, Michael? The acknowledgement that we have known each other before perhaps?

I never told you this, but although I had been planning to go to Vinexpo for over a year, there were moments this year when I said to myself, "I really can't afford this!" and *"Do I really want to go to a wine exposition?" I don't know why, but something made me go. I had this feeling that something would happen, or more specifically that I would meet someone who would have an enormous influence on my life. It was almost like a premonition. Through all of our fax correspondence prior to our meeting in Paris, I never even entertained the idea that it could be you. How naïve of me. By the time we got to Bordeaux, I was convinced I had met him.*

Did you make this happen, Michael? Did you really want me from the first moment we met two years prior? So much that your want for me made all of this become a reality? If so, then please don't stop dreaming, because I'm dreaming the same dreams now with you.

I miss you.

Barbara

The weeks went by and we would talk daily on the phone, and write long letters by night. But this soon became routine and I began to fear that he did not have the courage to jump ship completely. Time always seemed to be his excuse, and of course the logistics of selling his marital home and making sure his children were cared for were genuine reasons for the delay of an *action plan* for Barbara and Michael—but in reality, there simply didn't seem to be one.

***

Sacrifice

Having married so young, animal attraction is something I had never really understood until I experienced it post-marriage. It is said a woman is at her sexual peak in her mid-thirties, the benefit of years of experience being the aphrodisiac to the male species—apparently! Since leaving the marriage, most of my boyfriends had all been considerably younger, which I think also reflected my mental and emotional status at the time. I had not been looking for anything permanent, simply wanting to have fun. I was happy being a single mother, I loved having my own home, and I didn't want to share this with anyone. So what was I doing even entertaining the idea of a full time relationship with an older man? I had been there, I had done that.

The distance between us, coupled with the lack of an *action plan,* allowed doubt to grow and conspire against our dedication to be together. So, ironically, around this time of questioning, a young man began paying attention to me. The timing was really bad. Or was it? He was incredibly good looking, I might add. Sparks would ricochet off the walls and the pheromones were off the charts every time we encountered each other. He was another graphic designer, so we moved in the same social circles and became friends. Was he my own self-imposed test?

One night after another networking event, handy Andy and I became more than just friends. The flirting became furious, fueled by alcohol, so when he asked me back to his place I said "yes!"

The instant *it* was over I went into remorse overdrive. As I lay there afterward, wallowing in my remorse on the crinkled sheets, I thought to myself that I had broken something wonderful. Was it broken? Could I repair it? The sacred part I had gift wrapped in my heart was now soiled, and God how I felt it.

I raced home as quickly as I could, ran a bath and sat in

it until it went cold, contemplating what I had done and the ramifications of my thoughtless and reckless act.

Confusion churned like a murky sea. I had tested the waters with another man and I was quick to feel remorse at my own weakness. Even though there was not yet a fidelity agreement between Michael and I, why did I suddenly feel betrothed to him just because he had initiated the end of his marriage? But I believed fidelity was a voluntary thing and one of trust between two people, be they married or not.

I realized through this how much a person's thoughts play such an important part in the act of making love. If they're not in your head, then you're not there in body either. Michael had my mind as well as my heart and soul. Now, after I had tested my lust with another man, I wanted a covenant over my body that warded off predators. It didn't belong to anybody else. I wanted to be Michael's sanctuary.

But now I had a problem: to tell or not to tell?

I probably did not need to tell him. After all, how would he know, being twelve thousand miles away?

But I wanted to. Every aspect of our lives was linked through correspondence and I was acutely aware of the intimacy involved in sharing such an experience as this. It was more an admission of declaring the strength of love I felt for him than my weakness in going to bed with another man. This could not be done in a letter and so I called him to offer up my confession.

"Michael", my tone was different, anxious, and he picked up on it straight away.

"What's wrong?"

After a very long pause, he just knew and answered for me, "You've been to bed with another man haven't you?"

"Yes, I have. It meant absolutely nothing. If anything, it has only amplified the fact that what we have is unique and very special." I felt shallow in my attempt to disguise the mistake.

"It's okay. I understand, in a way. I didn't expect you to stay in every night waiting for me." He laughed a little, then added, "I only wish it had been with me."

"It really was just a case of too much alcohol, too much attention and that demon of being wanted and desired." This was something I knew was a very strong part of my make-up, and could always admit it.

"It's okay Barbara, I do understand and thank you for telling me, I appreciate your honesty".

God I wished he wasn't always so damned polite; it just made me feel more of a villain.

"Where are we now Michael, the whole incident has made me want you more and right now I just want to be in your arms"

"I don't know. I'm confused as well. I'll write to you and let you know."

I didn't expect to be absolved, so I accepted his terse sign off. I deserved it after all.

15th August 1995
My dearest Barbara,

It's a strange thing fate, isn't it? When I got to the office yesterday morning early, I nearly rang you at your office. It would have been around 4.30pm your time and I was thinking of you. I had woken very early, feeling a bit troubled, partly because I was going to phone my father to follow up my letter, and also because I wanted to phone the Australian office. Something, I don't know what, made me not phone you. Then I thought I would fax you a loving message, but was worried you wouldn't be there and the fax may be picked up by somebody else!

Then I thought of you saying that 6pm. your time was a good time to catch you, but at that time I was still on the phone and trying to come to grips with the horrors two weeks away from my desk had presented me.

Something seemed amiss and I was agitated. I could not really understand the feeling but I was suddenly worried about your feelings. It was almost like a premonition, but I put it down to my ongoing insecurity.

Sacrifice

Dear Barbara, I am sure I do understand your feelings, and I know how difficult it must be for you. My love for you has not diminished one jot. If anything it is stronger than ever, and to hear your voice on the phone this morning, expressing your feelings made me feel so close to you. I wanted to hold you to me, to surround you with my affection and understanding. How I crave the chance for us to get to know each other even better. If we can become so close in just one week, what does a lifetime hold? In one of your first letters, only six weeks ago, you said our love would have to stand considerable tests—distance, time, other people we meet, places we go, decisions we have to take— and you were right. Time and destiny will guide our thoughts and actions and our hearts will follow the path if we believe the course is right for us.

I went out for a walk at lunchtime today into the warm summer sunshine, bought a sandwich that I didn't really want and sat in the churchyard behind the office. I confess I felt sad and confused. To be perfectly honest, I also felt scared. It is not that I regret making the decision to end the marriage, I am perfectly at ease with that deep down. But I felt that my life was at a crossroad and I was frightened to take any of the paths, not just one of them. I thought about my children and how I may miss them growing up. I thought about losing the house and all that we have done to it to make it special, and the splitting up of the furniture and other possessions.

Then I thought about you, Barbara, the very, very special person who has come into my life and for whom I feel a kind of love the like of which I have never experienced before. I thought about wanting to be with you, not just for a week in Bordeaux, not just for a few days in Sydney or Adelaide, not just for a holiday in Tuscany, but forever. My mind raced to thoughts of being with you in Australia, of being proudly at your side when you're with your friends, of changing my life, my job, of leaving my family, my past. I know what my heart is telling me, and yes, it is scary!

Do you remember when we were in St. Emillion and I said that at times I go into churches for consolation, to sooth my troubled soul when it needs soothing? Well, I did just that. I popped into the empty church for some inner contemplation and reflection. Somehow, after a while, all seemed a bit clearer, and one can trust one's own sense of doing what is right! Later on this evening, I also had a session with Jackie, my aromatherapist, and it was a good opportunity for her to remind me of all the ways I must have faith in my higher self, to tell me what is right for me. I must reject any thought of guilt or feeling responsible for others. I must do what I want to do and everything else will fall into place. I must say, I feel so much better about everything now. I feel relaxed and the feelings of fear have disappeared. Also, the massage was just so (potentially) erotic. I was just wishing she would forget her professional status and let her

Sacrifice

hands (and mine) stray! However, it was not to be, and I just closed my eyes and imagined it was you massaging me—God it was good.

My darling, although I feel so close to you and trust my feelings, I do so wish I could see you again and be with you to explore you, your body and your mind, and for us to find out more about each other and what makes us 'tick'. I want my head to believe what my heart is telling me, and I want to take those risks. I suppose, being the insecure sort of person I am, I also crave the reassurance from you that you feel the same level of love and excitement. That is why I sometimes say on the phone how much I love it when you say, "I love you, Michael," in that special way you have. Just thinking about that now makes my spine tingle, and a smile breaks onto my face. I picture your face, your eyes, your mouth, and feel the warmth of your body close to mine, and I feel our needs, aspirations, strengths, and weaknesses all merge into one.

Despite all this, I also realize that your feelings may well change, given the difficulties of conducting such a form of long distance love affair and your changing circumstances. You must believe that I do understand, and that I will never bring any sort of pressure to bear on you. We must do what we feel is right for ourselves, as well as for each other, and if feelings change, or love's light dims, then we must not be frightened of saying so.

Having said all that, though as you said on the phone this morning, it is something special that we seem to have between us. No matter what happens in the future, I will always marvel at just how very special our love and mutual understanding is and how it developed in such a short space of time. Some things just seem so right, do they not? I just wish you were not so bloody far away. I want you so badly, it hurts. Even to hold your hand right now would be enough.

Thank you for your honesty and for telling me how you feel. I am jealous more of his opportunity to woo you and to give you love and attention. And I know how nice it is to receive those sorts of things, and even to feel them for somebody else. I know also what I can give you, and I believe it to be on a higher plane. Destiny, and our hearts, will decide whether that 'higher plane' will be the one that brings us together.

I wish you only the very best, and send you my fondest love. You have given me so much already and I am forever grateful.

Michael

His letter was full of so many contradictory statements. He also seemed to sign off like a farewell on a postcard rather than his previous urgency to be with me. Though he was totally understanding of the situation that had occurred, I sensed that I had placed him in a position of uncertainty with his own feelings.

A part of him wanted to seize the day and run with his heartfelt emotions. The other part of him was tied to his duty-

Sacrifice

bound responsibilities. I was fully aware of the time involved in needing to see his family secure and he kept reassuring me that it would not be long.

I expected him to feel hurt over my admission of lust, but his understanding nature made me realize that he was special indeed, and only confirmed that he was a deeply emotional person. I loved him more. The test drew me nearer to him.

Intensified somewhat by his aloneness now, he was halfway out of his marriage and I think he may have contemplated undoing all he had done.

August 29th 1995
Dear Michael,

How sorry I am to have put you through that. I did not mean to hurt you and know with certainty that it was my own test, but of course it has become yours as well.

We both knew that the distance between us would impose many issues in conducting a relationship. I guess this is just one of them?

As time goes on, and it has not been long, I have found myself distancing myself from Handy Andy as a friend so as to not mislead him any further.

He was starting to demand more of my time and I was just not prepared to give him this. We went for a walk last weekend and he started talking about our 'relationship,' at which point I reminded him that it was very presumptuous of him to even think that we were in one.

As I get older (and hopefully wiser), I think I am far more discerning about how I spend my time and with whom. In every instance I will opt for quality, quality and then more quality. There are no compromises, and in knowing what I like I am therefore creating my own environment, and inviting the right people into my life.

Consequently on Sunday, although I had already invited him on the walk, I did not want to be with him and therefore did not enjoy the day.

Human nature is a funny thing: lust is an emotion that tries us for sure, but once you have tasted the fruit and you know there is better, well it's all over red rover, isn't it?

Why stand in the aisle when you can have front row seats with caviar and champagne thrown in? Why drive a beaten up $500 Honda Civic when you can ride in an Audi? Why eat porterhouse when you can have Fillet Mignon served on the finest china, accompanied by the very best wine and finished with a Crème Brulée? So why bother indeed!

So I said goodbye to Handy Andy as a friend that day, never to be seen again.

No man has made me feel as womanly, wanted and desired as much as you have Michael. I miss

Sacrifice

you terribly, and as perverse as this may seem I am enjoying the sexual tension of the 'pain' of wanting you. It's deliriously strange but exciting, and I have never felt these feelings before.

Barbara

1st October 1995
My Darling Barbara,

 It's the first day of October—only one more calendar month to go until I board the plane that takes me to paradise! I can't tell you just how much I am looking forward to seeing you, despite our exchange of letters and faxes, with their expressions of love and deep feelings, despite our frequent and 'life saving' phone calls, I just cannot wait for the moment when I can hold you in my arms, look into your eyes and touch you.
 You've referred to our enforced separation as an aphrodisiac, and it's true that our feelings of love have intensified as the weeks pass. But at

times it can be painful. I suppose today was an example of how cruel the tyranny of distance and circumstance can be.

I know how much you love me, and this sustains me through the difficult times when I yearn to be by your side. I know also of how you 'tick' and how your sexuality, your ego, your physical needs and wants have to be recognized and fulfilled. We are very alike in some ways, and intriguingly different in others. Will it not be just so wonderful when there is someone there for you who can fulfill and satiate all your physical and emotional needs and wants?

It is this higher plane to which I keep referring and thinking, and I have never been so sure of anything in my whole life. I have thought and thought about many things over the past three months; marriage, children, job, environment, happiness, sadness, loneliness, love, sex, England, Australia. Each time I return to one inescapable thought and conviction: There is only one person in the world that I want to be with, and it's you, dear Barbara, the love of my life. I know that we have actually known each other for only a relatively short time, but it's an extraordinary feeling of conviction, with a mixture of faith and hope, that drives me to the same conclusion every time. While I am here, and you are there, and our contact is via poor phone lines or letters that take an age to arrive, it is perhaps difficult to see into the future.

My dream is that, come November 4th, and

Sacrifice

after the initial euphoric and emotional hours, we can learn more about each other and talk about the next phase, how we can turn our feelings of love and devotion into more concrete plans of a life devoted to fulfilling each others need's, into the merging of our souls, compensating for the lost years of unsatisfactory marriages, but looking forward also to a bright and happy future.

When I decided to write you this letter, I didn't want it to get too heavy, but to be honest I need to say the things I do, because it comes from the heart.

I move into my flat in 10 days. I wish it was sooner. It's not that life is difficult here, in fact the relationship between us is actually quite good, but I need to make the break properly, even though I know I will be a little lonely. I am looking forward to being in my own place for a while. There is still quite a lot more to be done on the separation issue, and I have yet to engage a lawyer, but I am hoping that we can avoid that at least for now.

She asked about you last night, and when I was going to see you. I fear she is envious of my having found someone with whom clearly I am in love. She said she wants only for me to find someone with whom I can be happy and fulfilled and sympathized with the predicament of our being apart. I hope too that she finds someone to give her what I could not.

Despite everything, we both agreed that we were each totally at ease with our decision to go our separate ways. In fact we are both a bit mystified as to just how relaxed we are about it! Thank God there is no animosity or hatred, and long may it stay that way.

Darling Barbara, I know the future at times seems uncertain, and that makes the present hard to fathom, but love is the fuel, destiny the map, happiness the reward.

I love you Barbara with an all consuming passion. I want you, but right now I miss you so much.

Michael

October 8th 1995
Dear Michael,

I have just come in from looking at the moon, and it is even more perfect tonight than last night's. Your phone call under the same moon made me feel so close to you and I can hardly wait until we are together again. I am especially looking forward to unleashing my love and passion upon you. To caress your head and stroke your neck to calm your fears as I did some four months ago, though I feel that you have overcome a lot of those fears

Sacrifice

already in that time.

Sometimes I wonder how often we will see each other during a year? By the time you arrive in November, it will have been five months since I last saw you, nearly half a year. I can't bear the thought of only seeing you twice a year; it's simply not enough, Michael!

Yes, I too replay my favorite bits (and there are many) of our treasured moments over and over in my head. I'd much rather have a relationship like this, with its intensity and beauty, than a mediocre full-time one. I'm not saying ours is not full-time, anything but. You know what I mean.

When you phoned I had just prepared a lamb shank casserole, which simmered all day and filled my house with the most glorious and appetizing aroma. I then attempted crème brulée (again) and think I may have perfected it. Was rather delicious and my boys loved it. I'm looking forward to cooking for you. Cooking is an expression of how I feel and I am finding myself wanting to cook more and more often, creatively I mean. You would not believe how bad my cooking had become in the later years of my marriage. I thought I had lost it! But it was simply just a part of me I had let go because I did not care anymore. I am now regaining that love of cooking through the contentment that comes from within.

By the time this letter reaches you, you may have already moved into your new flat. I realize it may be difficult for you. I found two books in my library I would like to loan to you. They were given to me by my friend Eileen, who is also from London and the same age as you. She is my Aussie 'sister,' and was my confidant throughout my marriage turmoil. (We all need someone to talk to every now and then). But books have been my constant companions of the past six or seven years, and I have used them as a source of comfort and inspiration. They have certainly educated me spiritually.

Oh, my divorce has come through! After the divorce decree we had a coffee together. My now official ex-husband wanted to have lunch, but I had to get back to the office for a twelve o'clock meeting. I sensed that he wanted to reflect somewhat on the happy years. I know that he has finally let go, but I felt that he was sad about it. After all it was twenty years to the day (today) that he asked me to marry him! I know that he was waiting for some sort of acknowledgement of the love we had from me, but I treated the whole procedure as if it was the end of a contract.

As I paused to cross the road he looked at me and asked, "a kiss for luck?"

Which I gave him and simply replied, "and we're on our way." They were the words to the song which was sung at our wedding; a song by Paul Williams, also sung by the Carpenters.

"We've only just begun to live...white lace and promises...a kiss for luck and we're on our way....."

As I walked away, I said to myself, "Don't look

back, never look back." My way of being stoic, I guess, because it did take me eight long years to instigate leaving, as he had always been able to emotionally coerce me into staying. If I did look back over my shoulder and had seen him standing there watching as I walked away... I don't know, Michael, perhaps I just didn't want to feel his pain any more. I'm on a new path now, with someone new...you!

Barbara

12th October 1995
My dear Barbara,

Well, here I am in my new flat—the transit stage between old and new. I am listening to the song 'All I Ever Wanted is You', most apt! I am tranquil, content even, despite the physical end to fifteen years of mixed emotions. It has been an extraordinary day, and now, a glass of cognac, a cup of coffee, your letter and books around me. I am happy with my flat; already it feels good to be *alone with my thoughts. The move has gone okay. I'll do more tomorrow when my brother comes up to help me. It was great to get your call, even though I was in the middle of the road carrying boxes from the car! Thank you for your thoughts and good wishes, they mean so much to me.*

My wife has been a great help and I admire how she is coping. I'm not sure exactly how she is feeling, though this is symptomatic of how little I really ever knew of her feelings. I think, like me, she feels relief tinged with sadness and some anxiety about the future (though I am very positive about my future happiness). Our primary concern has been for the feelings and well-being of the children. Up until now, both have responded incredibly well to the situation, and long may it continue.

Obviously today has been an important day for them, and we wanted to get the flat looking as homely as possible so that when they came around this evening they would be happy to see that I am going to be living in something nice and warm, rather than some hovel, which perhaps they had envisaged. Indeed it was an inspired idea, as they both were very happy with it, and quite excited. We went out, all together, for supper and I have just dropped them off, and here I am 'alone with you'. The thoughts of you and of us keep me going and inspire me. I feel such an inner peace the second I conjure up your image, recall your smile, read your words, imagine your body, and feel my soul

Sacrifice

caressing yours. I love you Barbara with a strength and to a depth that is seemingly unfathomable and I yearn to express it more tangibly.

In exactly two weeks from now I will already be an hour into my flight, and twenty four hours from holding you in my arms. Strap up your seat belt, start the countdown, the light at the end of the tunnel is getting brighter, the paths are getting closer, the metaphors are getting more bizarre! I'll see you in my dreams and beyond.

Michael

October 19th 1995
Dear Michael,

I have just received and read your letter accompanied by photos of your children. Your son is very much like you, isn't he? I can tell just by looking at them that you have a very close relationship. Both will naturally be very upset now that you have moved out of the marital home. Just be there for them Michael, until they come to terms with it all, at least. Still avail yourself to all the usual things you do with them, maybe *even more if possible. And then be prepared for the worst when one of them may turn on you! The one who instigates the move is always seen as the perpetrator of 'the end' in the eyes of the children. They just don't know that it takes the one with the most courage to do it!*

You write the most beautiful letters to me. I am afraid I need some fuel, like I had in Bordeaux, to reflect on paper to you. I am certainly desperate to have you physically in my life once more. That thought alone has been fuel, but I am running pretty close to empty.

I do so admire what you have done to date. You didn't have to move out before settlement, but I can understand your need to be alone with your thoughts too. How is the cooking going? I thought that you might like this recipe:

Take a juicy prime New Zealand lamb, inject it with creamy love, then marinate for five long months—she'll be 'ripe' mate! Tending and seasoning every now and then with dirty talk, very long phone calls which go beyond any reasonable persons budget, and photos of a tantalizing nature. After which the lamb should be succulent enough to pry open at the mere touch or a prick, and fall apart at the mere mention of a fork! She will then be ready...see you soon!

Barbara

Sacrifice

We were 'spotted' on Saturday morning by a friend of a friend, who said I was seen at Adelaide airport with my tongue halfway down a man's throat and my skirt halfway up my backside. I was fully aware of that moment, having deliberately worn a very short skirt and sexy underwear (a must have for an airport greeting with lovers), and in our first enthralling embrace I did lose my composure somewhat. Not that I really cared. The moment had almost been missed. I had arrived too late for his entry through the gates into the main lounge, missing the rush into each other's arms. Rather, I found him wandering and searching the hall for me. I just stood there till he recognized me, and then we merged and became truly one again.

"How the hell are you?" I asked.

"Much better now that I'm with you" he replied.

The five months of letter writing was the greatest aphrodisiac and we spent the majority of the first day making love. I had wondered if I would feel the same as I had in Bordeaux or whether I may even feel somewhat different. It felt euphoric to have him once again in my life, physically.

His trip, being a combined business trip, meant he was therefore obliged to spend a good part of the time in the Adelaide office working. I was amazed at the relative ease with which we slipped into a routine of normality. I loved having a partner again to attend dinners and social functions with, to just come home to and discuss our respective days over a gin and tonic. We did this anyway through our correspondence, even when we were apart, but being there certainly added a new dimension.

We were, in a way, consecrating all that had gone by in the intervening five months since we last saw each other. It was quite astonishing that the feelings fostered over a period of just one week could intensify to such devotion through simple letter writing. My belief in 'ordinary yet extraordinary' communication between a man and a woman had been reaffirmed somewhat with Michael. He offered me romance at a level of intensity never experienced before. We were able to initiate sex and loving wherever and whenever we desired, and to whichever the mood prescribed, and he offered me companionship and understanding.

***

After his week of obligatory work, I adorned my organizers hat for a sojourn away from Adelaide. We were heading southeast to Robe on the Limestone Coast, a major wine growing region that included Mt. Benson and Cape Jaffa, and then on to the Coonawarra and Padthaway.

The last time I had been to Robe was for the briefing to design the Cape Jaffa label, a family-owned operation who were in the fledgling stage of planting the first vines. In the early nineties there were many family vignerons who decided to value-add to their production by creating their own branded wine, rather than sell to the larger players who would dictate the price per tonne for their grapes. A situation that at first seemed out of their control eventually laid the foundation for numerous family-owned wineries, who in turn would become extremely successful wine producers during these halcyon years of the 90s.

I had met at the local Caledonian pub with the joint venturers; namely husbands, wives, sons, and daughters. There had been the obligatory ride in a rather dirty four wheel drive, usually through the vineyards, but in this case it had been over the bare hills to the spot earmarked for the intended cellar door. I liked this part of taking the journey with my clients. It was very relaxed, and the discussions in this particular case were over a pub meal and

Sacrifice

glass of wine where I tried to extract their vision for the pending brand.

No brief was ever given to me in this or other instances. I really can say that in those early years, the connection I had with the vignerons, culminated in label designs which were based on pure intuition. At this meeting, I clearly remembered asking for their wives' favorite colors as a staring point for my creation, and during that wonderful lunch I had a vision of how the label would look. This was, and remains, the only time I have experienced a 'vision' before embarking on the creative graphic process of designing a label, as if the whole look and feel of it had been given to me from a higher source.

I went straight back to Adelaide and created the Cape Jaffa label without any secondary options for consideration. I was convinced that they would like it owing to the extraordinary vision I'd had at our briefing session. That label is still in existence today, some twenty years later. We tried to tweak it years later in 2010, but could not improve upon it. A case of, *"If it ain't broke, don't fix it."*

***

The small seaside fishing village of Robe was our first port of call, an easy four hour journey by road. Situated on the coast at Guichen Bay, Robe is a popular holiday destination for families from both Melbourne and Adelaide. The main township has altered very little since the 19th century with many of the original stone establishments still standing.

There was a particularly lovely venue, The Criterion Cottage, where I had stayed during a family holiday ten years prior. When the renovated stone cottage was first opened we had been amongst the very first guests. I looked in the visitor's book, remembering that we had written our comments in it, and sure enough there were our names, and *"We'll be back for sure"*.

This episode, along with many others since, summoned me to a past that seemed to involve another person instead of me, a poignant reminder of the different person I was now. No longer a full-time mother and wife, I was now playing a role I had chosen for myself. One which suited me, but more importantly one I felt I was actively participating in.

We walked the sand dunes and beaches as if we were conjoined twins, ate simple pub meals with fabulous wines from the local district and dined every morning on Robe's famous *'dogtail sticky buns'* (a spiral, crispy, flaky yeast bun with a cinnamon and pecan nut center). Five months of waiting patiently for my lover to reappear in my life proved to me how good things come to those who wait.

But I kept questioning subconsciously, *"how would the relationship move to the next permanent level? How would the logistics make it happen?"*

He had a job in England, with no means to immigrate to Australia, unless…well, I wasn't even going to suggest that now, was I? Somehow, though, the logistics of our future did not seem that important. Living in the now did, and we were on cloud nine without a care in the world, sharing the euphoria we created by simply being together.

***

After two days in Robe we moved on to the nearby wine region of Coonawarra. Coonawarra's Terra Rossa soil is one of the most famous terroirs in the New World (of wine), a cigar like strip of

Sacrifice

rich red earth covering an area of just 15 kilometers long by 2 kilometers wide, home to thirty-three cellar doors that produce some of the best cabernet sauvignon in Australia.

We called in to visit some clients along the famous strip, and tasted wines at a chosen few to the point we thought better of driving the remaining distance back to Adelaide. The highlight of our stay, therefore, became an impromptu decision to stay at a grand Victorian mansion we stumbled upon at Padthaway. Situated in the middle of rolling vineyards, its grandeur and romantic charm seemed to draw us in. There is something quite delicious about being spontaneous, and the surprises that are encountered in this way.

There were only four other guests staying at the house, interstate motoring enthusiasts on their way back to Melbourne, their red Ferraris lined up graciously on the front lawn like grazing stallions. I decided to leave my little Mazda in the car park. Later, we joined the others after dinner in the drawing room for port and coffee, then adjourned to the billiard room for a game of pool.

After the first game of pool, the other guests retired to their rooms, which was a perfect opportunity for us to play up. I could tell he was thinking of some pretty wicked antics just by the look in his eye. So, while he was concentrating over his next shot, I slid up behind and gently lay my panties over his head. From then on it became more a game of chasing around the table, and near full-on sex, whenever it was my turn to sink a ball! I'm sure it was just beginner's luck because my concentration truly was elsewhere, but I sunk two balls in one hit, then a third (the last), and cleaned up the game with the black. It was a pure fluke but I felt like a real professional and it was exciting to beat him. Yet this was nowhere near as exhilarating as to what followed next.

Michael grabbed my dress and lifted it around my waist, then placed me on the table and made love to me. It was so grand being spread on a full-sized billiard table, taking my punishment for beating him in a man's domain. I left the panties in one of the pockets for the next player's inspiration.

***

Not all our trips were so wonderful, however. There were also the slightly disastrous sojourns that did not quite live up to our high expectations. As the travel taskmaster in choosing a variety of things to do, places to go, people to see, I had chosen the seemingly wonderful activity of hot air ballooning over the Barossa Valley, one of South Australia's other famous wine regions.

The flight was booked and paid for in advance, but it was only when the receipt and instructions arrived in the mail that I realized we had to arrive at the launch site before sunrise. The reason being once the sun comes up, the air becomes too turbulent for the balloon to take off. The conditions need to be absolutely calm for a successful balloon flight. I calculated that the location on their map was going to take us one and a half hours to get there, which meant getting up and leaving by 3:30am. to arrive before sunrise. Having paid an enormous amount of money for the privilege of the ride, we went to bed early. However, I am one of these people that just doesn't sleep if I know that I have to get up for something like an airplane flight, and ballooning fell right into that category.

Bleary-eyed, we headed north in my speedy Mazda to our destination, only to be herded like cattle into the back of an old Landrover of questionable quality, the sort that has metal bench

Sacrifice

seats facing the other passengers. No one seemed to be enjoying themselves just yet. Travelling the bumpy dirt tracks on those rigid cramped seats, with poor Michael barely fitting in and having to crouch down into a hunched position for the duration, seemed to take an eternity. When we arrived at the launch site, we were given the task of getting the balloons ready for take off. This involved arranging and holding the canvas out to aid the inflation process. While it was exciting to watch the flames gradually inflate and transform these colossus contraptions, somehow, in my mind, I had imagined that we would have simply arrived after a quick drive from Adelaide and hopped into the ready and waiting floating chariot for the hour's flight over the beautiful Barossa vineyards.

The *'champagne breakfast'* also left a lot to be desired. At least for the price we paid, I had expected white table cloths, directors chairs, fine flute glasses for the bubbles, and smoked salmon on rye bread. Instead, we were again trucked, this time to a public park, where we sat at fold-out picnic tables and drank cheap sparkling plonk combined with orange juice in plastic disposable cups, all delightfully served with dried fruit from Tupperware containers!

Maybe in Champagne France, we could have expected the first class amenities, but we made light of it and laughed like children, joking about it all the way home.

***

The two weeks we spent together, whether he went to work, on trips away, or generally just playing house, was a test, we knew, of the validity of our relationship moving into something more permanent. Sure enough, our feelings were still rock solid, the sex was getting better, and we both felt we had that special formula that made a relationships work. Pretty basic, fundamental stuff really. It was such a conundrum. While we were together, life was so normal, yet while we were apart our souls became exposed and vulnerable, and the relationship took on a certain mystical, pleasurable pain.

Slowly, the days leading to his departure back to England ebbed away. Aware, but not acknowledging that our time was limited, we cherished every waking moment we had. On our last evening together we decided to replicate the first evening we spent together in Bordeaux. The weather during the day had been in the low thirties, which I knew would lead into a typical balmy evening. A quick trip to the local deli had us set up in absolutely no time at all in my courtyard garden, basking in the warm November temperature, devouring the culinary delights with a fine wine.

One of the first things I fell in love with when I arrived in this wide brown land from New Zealand was the delight in wearing a sundress all day and into the evening without the need for layering up as night fell. I also loved the stark nature of the gum trees, which were so abundant, even in the cities. The trees were a super-highway for the many varieties of bird life. As with every sunset, the birds were now going nuts. Lorikeets squabbled, galahs squawked, crows cawed, and kookaburras laughed so loudly we could hardly hear ourselves over their cacophony, as if all for our pleasure.

We talked of the past two weeks, but we did not discuss the looming departure or even where or when we would next be together. There was no sadness, just the moment, and I guess that is all there ever is. To be this happy that nothing, not even the parting, was going to spoil *now*, amazed me.

Sacrifice

As the evening drew on and night fell, we lit candles and put on some lovely slow music. We shuffle danced around my tiny living room. I glanced into the window reflection and saw myself enveloped by this man, a man who made me feel so protected, not only from the world but from myself as well. I asked myself quietly, How could I lose myself so utterly in a man to this point? This wanting and yearning for him, especially after my own long search for my true self and subsequent independence: How did I get here?

I was a paradox unto myself! But the knowledge of a secure and loving relationship calmed any uncertainty as to how or when our relationship would become permanent. We simply didn't discuss the next stage, feeling that it might spoil our euphoria. The how and when we would see each other again were mere details. We both seemed to have faith that destiny would carry us along this path, and eventually we would be together forever, somehow.

***

19th November 1995 (Somewhere in the sky)
My dear Barbara,

Only 3 hours since I last saw you, touched you, smelled you, kissed you, and all of me aches with longing. The last two weeks have only served to confirm that which I knew—that our love is special, intense, honest, and strong. I have been happy beyond the level I thought possible, and I thank you deeply for making me that way, and for taking me into your life.

I want to be a part of it and to enhance it. My journey will be hard on my emotions, but the destination is clear and inviting. Much of what needs to be done only I can do, but I know I can count on your help, support, guidance, advice, and love. I value your love and friendship very, very deeply.

Your messages, in my books, are lovely. So apt, and gentle. They inspire me. Thank you once again for such a happy time that will tide us over until our next meeting.

My personal video screen, which has more functions and channels, both audio and video, *than you could possibly imagine, informs me that there are just 21 hours to go before we land in London. A copy of The Times from Saturday takes great delight in showing a picture of the first heavy snowfalls causing traffic chaos to the north of England. Doubtless with the wind coming off the Arctic, this winter horror will hit London any day now!*

The journey has been uneventful, even comfortable. There's no doubt that business class these days give you more room and relative comfort than I remember even from a year ago. I've not said more than three words to my adjacent companions (both Australians) and I have flitted between reading Bill Bryson, watching boring videos, sleeping, but mostly listening to music and staring at the ceiling recalling and recounting and reflecting on two of the happiest weeks of my life (so far).

My recollections are of a period when time seemed to stand still, and when emotions were charged to a level I hardly dared consider possible. The memories of what we did together and how we felt, what we said, how we laughed, the passion of our lovemaking, the joy of our being together, just make me smile out loud (can you smile out loud?). I fear also they bring a lump to my throat and tears to my eyes. Happiness and sadness, laughter and pain, are sometimes so closely related. The happiness of the memories is counter-balanced by the sadness of our separation. The laughter that I recall so vividly is sometimes wickedly stifled by the pain of not being able to hear you laugh (for a while) and when I realize the tasks ahead.

But I am genuinely awakened from my sad thoughts by the burning desire to hasten the moment when we can continue the beautiful journey we have started, to continue to taste the fruits of desire and sheer happiness that we have provided for ourselves.

The future, my future with you, is in a land I have visited, tasted, enjoyed, and embraced. And that land is eminently reachable and I can't wait! I have experienced a level of love and contentment without complacency that has enriched me deeply. My love for you has grown, my yearning for you has strengthened. Yes, my dear darling Barbara, you are my friend, my lover and soul mate. How much I look forward to adding one more title to that list...

Take care my love. No matter how far away I seem, I am constantly at your side.

All my love,
Michael

Sacrifice

*Too long a sacrifice.......
can make a stone of the heart.*

William Butler Yeats

CHAPTER 3

Negativity Lands

[Adelaide - London - Côte d'Azure - Dec 1995 / Feb 1996]

The past week since Michael left had been interesting in that my boys had visited me every evening and also wanted to stay over more than usual. Their father had started a relationship with a new woman, and I suspected they were not that happy about it. Or perhaps they had missed me during my private two weeks with Michael and sensed a rival for their affections. I always tried to be very upbeat for them, in a role model sort of way. I did not consider myself to be a conventional mother by any stretch. I had not included them on any activities with Michael and me, and chose to introduce them on a more cordial occasion over a home-cooked meal. Children being what they are, hated him instantly, but I half expected this, which is why I did not push the boundaries of initiation during his stay. I knew we did not need to encounter the negatives just yet, so early in our union.

My eldest son was going through a very assertive stage, which I thought was good for him (he had always been very quiet and withdrawn throughout his early childhood). My younger son was revealing a lot of frustrations to me and I sensed he held me partly responsible for his current misery. Each evening he would ask for a photo album to view, which I obligingly provided. I hoped that viewing the memories and the reflection they would induce might provide him with a sense of fulfillment, in at least knowing that his early childhood had been a happy one. For most of it I know it was. I had always been an ardent photographer, compiling the many albums of our memories together, and had kept them after my husband and I parted. I had given him a couple of albums from the later years. The hardest one to part with was the wedding album, perhaps because this was all I could leave him of the promises we had made to one another. However, I wanted to keep the commemoration of our twenty years together; it was a visual record of our time together and an important stage of my life, as a wife, but especially as a mother to my young sons.

On this Tuesday night, we looked at the pregnancy and his birth photos, which triggered some bizarre dreams that night. Dreams in which I was nine months pregnant and then became overdue. In the overdue weeks the baby stopped kicking and I knew that it had died, yet I didn't want to tell anyone. I didn't want to face the truth. I knew the consequences would be going through the trauma of delivering a dead baby and I would never be able to face having any more children. It was a powerful dream and I woke feeling incredibly sad.

Was the pregnancy my marriage, could I just not go there again knowing that the gestation period always ends? Was this a warning, a premonition that I was about to repeat the past and make the same mistake?

I had another dream the following night; I was inspecting a house for sale in Wellington, New Zealand, my home town. The couple that owned the house appeared to be very distant, yet the wife appeared pregnant. There was also a daughter, who just happened to be an old school friend of mine. The house was also very similar to my marital home. It was very ugly outside, but light, airy and large inside. During the inspection of the house, I asked if it had a cellar and the couple confirmed that it did. As I climbed down into the cellar I found myself saying, "I had a cellar once, too."

Was the location of my home town an indication that I did not need to go back there, and in fact leaving home and country at 17 was a pretty good indication that I was an adventurer seeking novelty rather than a conformity? Was the house also a representation of my past marriage and commitment, and the cellar simply a dungeon, a prison without the bars? Our marital home had a wine cellar too!

The recent dreams were disturbing and caused me to question everything I was doing. Were the dreams my subconscious talking to me, telling me to wake up?

December 30th 1995
My dear Barbara,

So here we are at the end of 1995, an eventful year. A year during which I discovered a very special love—one that enriched my life, captured my heart, gave me the power to break free and feast my eyes on fertile pastures and unbounded happiness. Meeting you, Barbara, and the realization that I loved you, were, without doubt, the high points of my life so far.

It's as if my life, my heart and my soul were trapped in a deep dark cellar, with only a tiny glint of light coming through a skylight—out of reach. You came along and your being shone through the skylight, forcing the bars apart, reaching down, encircling me, lifting me up, giving me the strength to rise up and escape through the bars, out of the cellar, into the warm embracing sunlight.

I'm not quite out in the open just yet—there are still a few walls to climb and rivers to cross—but at least I can see you and you are there encouraging me and giving me the strength, the reason, the incentive—I can feel the adrenaline.

Thank you, dear Barbara, for being the One for me! For teaching me to break the rules, for giving me the courage. I think of an old Tibetan proverb, "It is better to have lived one day as a tiger than 1,000 years as a sheep!"

I've just re-read the last 2 pages and realized it's all a bit heavy—sorry about that!

Anyway I know you don't mind it when I describe my feelings and emotions, just as I love it when you do. It's the intensity of our feelings that helps to make it all so special—and it's been that way since June 1995, right from the start.

Thank you for giving me that very special gift of intimacy. I treasure it, and value it hugely. Mi casa es su casa.

Yours,
Michael

Sacrifice

In realizing that the relationship was moving very much toward the sort of conjugal familiarity to that which I had known in my marriage, I wanted Michael to know that there were other realms of possibilities for self-expression. I was teaching him. I had opened up my heart to him, therefore giving him the strength to move forward with his life.

I found it curiously bizarre that he used the same analogy of the cellar I had in my dream. He referred to it also as a dark prison from which he had emerged. I had not told him of my dream, fearing it would be to obvious an interpretation of my fears of commitment to the sort of relationship we were developing.

He had been able to sense when something happened with me, such as the night I hooked up with Handy Andy. Did we have a telepathic connection that defied the distance between us?

Yet I began to question whether this relationship was going to survive the tyranny of distance, and just how many more letters could we write to sustain the love. Indeed, how many more ways with words could we reinvent and express our feelings?

In life itself, without ideas there can be no progress, and in the long run survival depends upon creativity. Creativity requires risk, and living with the energy of inventive ideas and creating new ways of living through sheer imagination. I therefore put myself out there and began to write erotica!

Considering fantasies need to be taken in context, and I am writing erotica from a woman's perspective, one of the many things I will acknowledge first and foremost is that men and women are different, especially where our hormones are concerned. In my view there are three types of sex: mechanical sex, playful sex and mind sex.

Mechanical sex is where the function is so predictable you could set your clock to it. You know just which buttons to press to make them tick and exactly how long it takes for the alarm to go off. This is always performed in exactly the same place and usually the same position. Some people like mechanical sex, but they usually have the same cereal for breakfast every day and wear the same brand of underwear for life as well.

Playful sex is how we get to know each other. I should have put it first because mechanical sex is what playful sex usually evolves into, once two parties unite in marriage. Playful sex involves getting to know your partner and their boundaries. As no two couples will ever be able to create anything like what another couple may produce. This playful involvement is anticipated with excitement as it sets the groundwork for mutual trust and understanding for the new couple. This usually involves inventive positions, clothing accessories (worn by either partner so long as it makes you laugh or turns you on), and acted upon spontaneously whenever the urge arises. I have to emphasize here that playing makes you happy and that there is no greater aphrodisiac than laughter!

Mind sex is what you experience when you are basically on your own, and all you have is your imagination. Mind sex does not exclude physical sex, for you can have it alone, or with a mechanical or playful partner. I have always thought that the realm of fantasies should remain just that. We are able to create such wonderful characters in our heads, but when we try to replicate them in reality, it's hard for any real person to live up to one's own florid imaginings.

So, alone again in our separate worlds, with only words to comfort, soothe… and to have sex with!

Along comes Desireé.

Sacrifice

DESIREE DANCES IN RED STILETTOS!

He had not seen Desireé for well on a year, but thought of her often with a lust that was... well, quite uncontrollable. She was so god damned expensive though...but worth every Franc. And so he calls her, and requests her delicious services.

"Michael," she says, "so good to hear from you. I had been thinking of you lately and wondering when you would call. What would you like?"

"I want you to strip for me," he replies.

When she arrives, he offers her a drink and they sit and chat quietly, demurely, knowing of the erotic desires about to be unleashed between them. She asks him to remove his shirt so that she can be aroused by watching him too (half-naked men are so sexy). She is wearing a long black wrap-around skirt, a slinky black silk blouse and red patent leather stilettos.

The music and dance begins. For the first track, Enigma; he just watches her move, de-lighting in her fully clothed body. Anxious to see her again after such a long time. She slowly opens her skirt to reveal her red panties. Running her hands over the insides of her thighs, she asks Michael to untie the *skirt and in one swift movement it is gone. With her back to him she unbuttons her blouse, the G-string revealing her extremely tight derrière and the red stilettos accentuating her exquisite legs. The open blouse exposes Desireé's small breasts (well perhaps they could be large, in the fantasy, just for a change) as she fondles her nipples, making them very erect.*

Desireé is enjoying watching Michael become aroused...evident by the way his pants are fitting better. She removes her little panties, exposing a freshly shaven pussy, which she rubs slowly, fondling her breasts with the other hand. She gives Michael a taste by coming very close and beckoning him to try. Such a tease—he is only allowed one lick! Slowly the blouse is removed and Desireé dances provocatively for a whole track, totally naked except for the lovely red shoes. He delights in her body, wants her so badly, aches for her.

She finishes the dance lying on the floor and begins to touch herself slowly, then more vigorously. It does not take long to climax. He watches her arch her back and cry out with delight as the waves of release ripple through her body. He is on the floor next to her wanting to penetrate and release his animal desires he has for this creature. He wants to fuck like crazy and devour her body, but she wants to tease just a little more, push him to the brink.

She commands him to lay on the floor naked, then ties his hands to a chair leg as punishment

Sacrifice

because he can't keep his hands off her and she had instructed him not to touch! She stands up, still in those red stilettos, and straddles him, walks the length of his body, then back again. She lowers herself down onto his face. He's so hungry for her that he can't get enough. Desirée is so excited that her second orgasm comes within seconds and she has to pull away.

Now it's his turn. While her fingers probe and fondle him, she takes him in her mouth. He still can't touch her, as his arms are totally bound above him. Feelings of helplessness, ecstasy and lust pervade his senses as he climaxes in huge waves into her mouth, then all over her breasts.

She glides away, smoothly slipping up his body and says gently as she unties him, "Don't leave it so long 'till the next time—au revior, á bientot darling"!

"Tout mon amour, Desireé."

"PS: That will be five thousand Francs. Merci!"

28th January 1996
My dear Barbara,

What a lovely transition from dream to reality! Thank you for sending over the warmth of your voice to cut through the ice that's on the window panes. Nothing could be finer than to be awakened by such soothing.

I do so enjoy my frequent 'fixes' when I get to talk to you on the telephone as I did this morning. Each time I ring off (which is not easy to do) I just sit there smiling quietly to myself, and I feel on a high. I do so love the effect you have on me. I love the way you make my prick so hard—even when you're not here! Don't ever stop.

Here's mine: You and I are in a bar chatting, drinking with friends. You are looking gorgeous and sensual, wearing your suede short skirt (the one you wore to meet me at the airport) and top which shows the contours of your delicious breasts—I can just determine your nipples beneath the fabric. At this point we are not together, you are talking to someone else, but I catch your eye from across

Sacrifice

the room. Our eyes greet each other but our faces display nothing. All I do is nod towards the door and I leave.

I go down the street and turn into a dimly lit alley. Some paces behind, you follow. As you pass, I catch your arm, pulling you towards me—no words are spoken. In one swift motion I pull your top clean over your head and off. Your breasts quiver as I run my hands all over them, tweaking the nipples roughly. How proud they stand, how good they feel. Your head is thrown back in anticipation, suddenly I reach up under your skirt and grab hold of your panties in both my hands and just rip them apart. With my knee I force your legs apart and with one hand I feel you whilst the other hand reaches into my trousers to release my hard, aching, hot prick and with one swift action I impale you hard against he wall. The force of my penis thrusting up inside you actually lifts your whole body off the ground. You can feel the hard, cold bricks of the wall on your naked back. Your arms are around me and can feel the heat of my body even though I'm fully clothed. You lift both legs off the ground and clamp them around my waist as I continue thrusting forward and upwards passionately, whispering in your ear that you are the most fantastic creature that ever walked this earth, swearing my undying love for you even though I am fucking you up against a wall as if we were total strangers. With one final powerful thrust I come with an incredible intensity.

> *We go back to the bar for another drink with a smile teasing the corners of our mouths. Just thinking about fucking you makes me hard for you Barbara. How I just wish we were together now. I so miss your body and being close to you. I don't know how I am going to last another couple of months. Clothed or naked, in Adelaide or in London, in 1995 or in 1996 and beyond—you are my fantasy, Barbara. It will come true, I know it. I have been listening to Enigma whilst writing this letter. The tracks are incredibly erotic, you know, lots of heavy breathing. She's just sung, "Prends moi, je suis à toi mia cupla." (Take me, I'm yours, the guilty one.)*
>
> *Prends moi, Barbara, Je suis à toi.*
>
> Yours always
Michael.

Well, this put a whole new perspective on the relationship. I was intrigued however at the vast diffference between the male and female ideas of *fantasy*, as Michael's were, well, almost violent! So opposite. But thats what we are right, the *opposite* sex. Desireé was developing quite a liking for Michael. Barbara had some competition brewing!

***

BLUE SUEDE SHOES

We're in a hotel room, it is cold, grey, wet and misty....but we're warm in there. The hotel is very opulent with traditional touches to the rooms, marble bathrooms and brocade bedspreads, very fitting for a Lord.

"Shall I call her now?" I say, as I slowly undress to my electric blue undies, which match my electric blue suede stilettos.

"Yes, hello. I wish to request the services of Delicious Desireé... Yes, that's correct. We know she is the most expensive you have. Thank you very much."

The doorbell rings and she is here! You are under strict instructions to sit and watch only. I smile at her when I answer the door, introduce myself and guide her into the room, introduce you to her.

"Desireé, this is Michael..."

Before I can finish, she quickly interrupts.

"Yes. I know, we have met already"

You watch me undress her, and as I do, I gently fondle her breasts and run my hands all over her beautiful body. When she is completely naked. I *stand and fondle her breasts in every way I'd like to have mine fondled. I rub mine against hers, suck them, flick them, tease and cup them in my hands. I don't let her touch me. I'm terribly aroused, and intrigued by feeling another woman's body. I then instruct her to undress you and give you head. I watch...You are so hard, but not allowed to touch her! She has to do it all to you. She is an expert at fellatio, and I'm picking up lots of tips! I can see by your excitement that it is not going to take long, so I slide up beside you in your chair and let you fondle my breasts. I kiss you passionately, my tongue fucking with yours. I can feel you coming, and as you do she takes you all in her mouth, swallowing every drop. I thank her and pay her, sending her off. I want you to myself now. I'm so aroused I know I will come far too quickly. It is only minutes since you blew, but already you're hard at the thought of fucking me. On the bed, you lick my entire body like an animal savoring his prey for a final tantalizing meal, and finally I feel your cock penetrate my body. The tease has been so delicious, and writing this makes me want you so badly right now.*

Erotically yours,
Barbara

Sacrifice

All I needed was an excuse to see Michael again. He offered it by inviting me to a formal dinner put on by his posh, exclusive gentleman's club held annually in February. Every year they alternated invitations being offered to female and male guests, and this year was the year of the female! I think he half-expected me to refuse, because of the ludicrous idea of flying all that way to the UK for a dinner. But I was feeling impulsive and I kind of liked the crazy idea, so I went out and bought a ticket to London.

It had been three and a half months since we had been together. But the intervening months had shed a new perspective on our relationship. We'd left each other in November with tender warm memories of each other. This, enhanced by abstinence, and erotic letter-writing was a recipe for explosive sex, which is exactly what it was. The intensity of pleasure felt with Michael quite often left me in tears—the heady mixture of erotic sex and love overwhelmed my senses. He'd ask me what was wrong when this happened and I could only reply, "Nothing is wrong, everything is just perfect."

I felt more sexual and womanly than ever before, and he never tried to control me. In fact, he reveled in my need to express myself sexually. In a way I think I was erasing his preconditioned ideas of a man's responsibility and need to perform and control in the bedroom.

***

The formal dinner at the gentlemen's club required white tie with decoration for the gentlemen and evening dress for the ladies. We made such a handsome couple. I so enjoyed being at his side, his partner, his lady. Moreso, I enjoyed who I was when I was with him.

I had never yet had the occasion to dress up in Australia like this, but loved doing so nonetheless. I had recently bought a dress on a whim, knowing full well I'd probably only wear it once. It was a tight navy blue slinky number which exposed my midriff through a soft navy net. This also discounted the possibility of wearing underwear! I knew it was far too risqué and inappropriate for the occasion, but I liked the thought of my minor rebellion to the British establishment. This would also be the first time Michael would be seen with a woman other than his wife. I wasn't seeking approval, and I certainly did not want to conform to anyone else's ideals. Michael would just have to cope with my individuality (and if he did think the dress was improper, he never let on).

The evening's proceedings were one long parade of pomp and ceremony, with some quirky British customs like kidneys after dessert. Mine naturally went untouched.

Because 1996 was leap year, and this particular event was held was the 29th of February, it was also traditionally a day when a woman could ask a man to marry her. Michael was seated directly opposite me. I hadn't planned it at all, and just came out with it. "Michael, will you marry me?"

This prompted a stuffy silence from the guests around us that you could cut the air with a knife. They all waited in anticipation for his response. Quite literally put on the spot, he took no time at all in deliberating his reply.

"Why yes, I'd be delighted to Barbara."

We both smiled wryly at each other knowing full well it was just a leap year joke, than actually tying the knot, but we certainly gave everyone on the table something to gossip about—especially considering Michael's still-married status.

We never discussed the proposition again during my visit.

Sacrifice

In fact we never discussed the future, or logistics around being together eventually, at all.

***

The following day we headed off to the South of France. Michael's flat was above a shop in the main street, with no parking facilities, so we'd taken all the bags down to the street, ready to load into the car. As I waited with the bags, I had the distinct uneasy feeling that I was being watched. It was very unnerving, but I was positive that Michael's wife was close by, just observing me. Sure enough, while we were packing the car she drove by and stopped, the window slowly slid down. She turned to me and our eyes met, the moment of curiosity finally satiated for her.

"Have a nice time, won't you?" she said.

I wondered if she really meant it, and how she must have felt watching her cooler, luggage and husband being packed up ready for a romantic sojourn in the South of France with another woman. I smiled and said "thanks," but she didn't smile back.

I couldn't believe I was back in France in less than a year. But then, since meeting Michael, my whole life seemed to be filled with magic and all sorts of possibilities. Our destination was Collobriéres. A friend of Michael's had an apartment in this town, and although it was not the Côte d'Azur it was an easy one hour drive to the towns of St. Tropez and Nice, and two hours further on to Monaco. The town of Collobriéres itself was almost deserted, and we wondered whether it came to life in the summer months or if it was in danger of becoming a ghost town.

The French determined their own hours of shopkeeping, and we'd sometimes go out to buy baguettes at some ridiculously sane hour like two in the afternoon, only to find the one deli in town closed. The butcher shop was out of another era, and had cuts I'd never seen before, but the beef and lamb was the best I'd ever tasted. The town seemed locked in a time warp, as if we'd stepped back fifty years. Even the residents were ancient. We seemed to lower the average age some forty years with our presence in the town.

It was still winter, however being that much farther south than England made all the difference in the day's temperature. Most days were a balmy 15 Celsius, but one of the best aspects of the South of France during the winter months was the distinct lack of tourists. We'd set out on day trips to the coast, then return late in the day and settle into the apartment, open a bottle of wine and cook the evening meal. I marveled somewhat at the ease with which we enjoyed each other during the day, and how we transposed into sexual demons at night.

After our four days exploring the coastal towns on the Côte d'Azur, we began our return trip to England, meandering north through Burgundy, hugging the Rhône River for most of the way. There was no hurry. The super highways, which we avoided, didn't offer the spectacular scenery or intimate towns of the country roads. We had screamed down the autoroute last week in order to arrive at our destination quickly, but now we could take our time and enjoy the French countryside. It was intriguing to see how the French vineyards grappled steep, rocky hillsides, in comparison to Australia's gently rolling hills and wide open spaces.

Michael was determined to find a certain hotel he'd stayed at years previously. He remembered its upmarket qualities and great location, right on the Rhône, but couldn't remember the town. Yet find it he did, after exhaustive attempts liaising with shop owners.

I liked the way we spontaneously took each day as it occurred, not planning too much, and happening upon an idea like staying at the upmarket hotel on the Rhône as we drove along. Michael was always so attentive and kind, and his sense of humor gave him a combination of the most attractive traits I could find in a person. He ran me a hot bubble bath, and once in it, produced the gin and tonic.

After the most splendid dinner in the most elegant of settings, accompanied by a rare vintage local wine, the mood was set for an evening of more delicious fun. That night he asked for the services of Desireé!

"But Michael," I replied, "she must remain a fantasy, as fantasies are just that, our imagination!"

"I just want to meet her, what harm is there in that?"

Wearing a black trench coat with satin lining covered in roses, black stilettos (yes, I always carry an "emergency" pair), and nothing underneath but lacy burgundy silk lingerie, she arrived at the hotel room and knocked.

"You requested my services, monsieur?" she said, as she seductively strode past him. "What is your request this evening monsieur?"

"Well, firstly I'd like to observe the merchandise" he replied.

Slowly, and with her gaze holding his, she untied her belt, then unbuttoned her coat and parted the fabric to expose her semi-naked body. She lost his gaze at this point, as he reached for her, tracing every curve of her body with both of his hands.

"There is to be no kissing" she instructed. "It's against the rules."

We both laughed, because we knew there were no rules. He slid the coat off her shoulders and let it fall to the floor, and then instructed her to remove the underwear. She did so, obligingly, and ever so slowly.

Desireé stood naked, apart from the black stilettos, in front of her client, while he undid his trousers and produced his hard, erect penis and began to massage it.

He instructed Desireé to sit on the writing desk while he undressed himself. He devoured her body in kisses, but their lips never met. When he entered her, the penetration felt like the magic of first-time sex with a new person. After all, Desireé was a new woman. We made love for what seemed like hours on the writing bench, the ecstasy for us both I'm sure was more cerebral, or perhaps it was the combination, but when he cried out, "Oh God Barbara, don't ever leave me," I didn't reply. I had lost myself. I was Desireé.

***

The following week spent in London was a total contrast to our time in France. I was prepared for Michael's need to work, or at least put in an appearance. I was only too pleased to amuse myself during the day, and looked forward to his company immensely in the late afternoon. But it was disconcerting to see his character change in his native environment. He was reserved, withdrawn and focused entirely on himself.

The first evening back, I remember in particular, I prepared one of my favorite meals and was relishing the thought of an intimate evening together. After all, part of building any relationship is the *little things*. I listened with keen interest to his busy day and all the details of the problems at the office, until my keenness wore thin, through neglect on his part. He paid no compliment to the meal I had prepared with love, and the

Sacrifice

playing house routine suddenly felt twenty years old. I started to remember my marriage and how the complacency had slowly snuck in. This was so sudden! I wasn't ready for the abrupt descent from holiday romance to reality, and I wondered for the first time if we had been living in dreams whilst *on location*. What had prompted it?

Every evening that week, Michael revealed a portion of his past to me in the form of photographs. I think the albums were the most poignant insight to his past and certainly his marriage. Photographs, and their chronological assembly, had become somewhat of a ritual in my life. My ex-husband had always commented on how beautifully and thoughtfully I had placed our lives into perspective through photographs. At the end of our twenty-year marriage, one of the hardest things to divide up was the albums, as I have already mentioned. The memories were more precious than any furniture or real estate, and they were perhaps how we came to part so amicably; we had created a beautiful life together, even though it had come to a close. I believed that my assembly and organization of the photos was an adytum to the institution of our family and what we had created. I can remember how eagerly I awaited the photo processing after holidays, so that I could visualize the contents in an orderly sequence. It was deeply satisfying to see my life, my children's lives and my family in a growing visual format.

Volume upon volume upon volume. At the end I think there were about fifteen albums, almost one for every year of my marriage. The photo-taking had naturally lessened as the children got older, but the albums never stopped. Nor have they. Three years into my new life, I proudly boast five, and one was dedicated entirely to Michael and me.

While Michael slowly revealed his past, I asked why his wife had not wanted to keep any of the albums, for I knew she had been the one who had catalogued their fifteen years together. The fact that she had not wanted any of the albums, and had passed them all over to Michael, was an indictment in itself. I felt a deep empathy for her, for in the photos I saw myself, young and vibrant. But the vast difference between us was that I had been loved, and still had the memories I cherished and held on to. In viewing Michael's photos, I couldn't help but assume her perspective and felt the deceit of all those years. I couldn't tell why they never loved each other, but I found myself feeling sorry for her.

Michael had hoped to introduce me to his children and was excited at the prospect, but they were upset about my being in England, perhaps about my very existence, and did not wish to meet me. I was completely at ease with this, and felt that it was too soon after the separation for them to have to cope with meeting the woman who was theoretically taking their mother's place in their father's life.

I don't believe children should be forced to deal with issues they are not ready for. I did not want to see them suffer their own mixed emotions, and I felt sad that my simply being in England had upset them. His wife also had suddenly become quite bitter about the existence of another woman, whereas in the first instance she was relieved her marriage was over. Stupidly I had hoped we could one day be friends.

Only four of Michael's family members cared to meet me, his two brothers and their respective wives, but it was painfully obvious that they felt uncomfortable. So did I. Michael had kept his unhappy marriage a well-guarded secret, in true British tradition, so his separation came as somewhat of a surprise to his immediate family.

Sacrifice

Our last day together was gray and dismal outside, and the mood inside was not that much brighter. We had planned to go into London and have a late lunch at Ransomes Dock, where we had gone some eight months earlier. Because the weather had turned nasty, so I stated that I didn't care much whether we went or not. Michael watched a rugby match on TV while I packed. I would rather have gone to bed for the entire day to make love. I guess my impending departure had sullied both of our moods.

Or was it something else?

***

The week in London had planted my feet firmly on the ground and I began to question a lot of aspects of the relationship. One was his changed persona on home territory. He seemed like another person, which I tried to shrug off and put down to job difficulties and the surrounding family issues of the past week. Nevertheless, I felt a mixed sense of relief and regret when I departed Heathrow. Relief that I was going back to Australia's brilliant summer, and regret that I did not talk about these new feelings with him.

I was always aware of the fact that we had spent very little physical time getting to know one another, and that the time we did spend was always on holiday, and therefore not real life situations. Perhaps I had just experienced reality and for the first time since the relationship began, and I now questioned our compatibility.

I could also sense his weakening resolve and realized that not once during the past two weeks had we discussed future plans or his strategy to disentangle himself from England and his family. There had been a certain amount of fallout with his employers, caused by his recent job searching in the Australian wine industry—they feared he might depart for Oz any day—and had offered him a twelve month contract, which he accepted. I would have expected this kind of confinement to spur him to reach for freedom, but instead he clung even more tightly than ever to his sure ties in England. I wondered if he would ever really be able to make the break. When he told me of his fears of possibly losing his job, the Audi, and all the other perks that went with it, I realized that he still had a long way to go with his own self-belief before he'd be able to sever the apron strings to the motherland and a life he claimed to dislike so much.

Consequently, upon my return to Australia, I fell into a deep depression, born of the confusion in being so tightly bound emotionally to him and my fear of mediocrity in our developing relationship. I became sick with laryngitis and lost my voice completely, which I'm sure was in direct response to how my fractured soul was feeling. During my incubation in bed, I felt alone and confused. The elated experience of our romantic holiday in France, fighting with the negative feelings of the last week in London, forced me over the brink into the abyss of darkness. Had I subconsciously created this tense, unpleasant situation through my fear of complacent relationships? Had I attracted this so that I could learn how to deal with that fear, that terror?

I was in a very dark and hellish place. I felt lost and I cried out for help. I sent out a plea of help to the Universe. It was the first time in my life I'd actually prayed, and understood it.

Sacrifice

*To thine own self be true;
and it shall follow as the night the day,
thou canst not then
.....be false to any man.*

William Shakespeare

CHAPTER 4

We lose direction

[USA San Francisco - April / June 1996]

As if by magic, my prayers were answered the very next day. I received a call from a design company in the USA that also specialized in wine label branding, wanting to discuss the prospect of my working for them. I'd been headhunted!

Owing to the depression I'd sunk into since my arrival back from England, the job offer seemed just what the doctor ordered. I needed to break out of my rut. I also felt professionally jaded, and the daily grind of doing it all by myself as a freelance consultant was getting to me. The thought of having someone else communicate with clients, deal with the mundane invoicing and chasing of money, leaving me the luxury to just design appealed to me very much. I was also creatively lonely, and I relished the thought of working with other designers in a team environment. The job would be a chance to view my life from a broader perspective, away from my business, my kids, my friends, my house, my ex-husband, and of course daily contact with Michael. The Universe had thrown me a big fat curve ball. It was an opportunity I just knew I had to pick up and run with. This was a gift.

Before I had left for the last trip to England and France, a professional colleague had asked me if he could take samples of my work over to the USA to show a San Francisco design company. I didn't know they were looking for talent, but that's how the offer came to be. I was elated, and said, "Yes, I'll go!"

In all respects it seemed like a perfect opportunity to experience working for someone else, and doing so in a foreign country was an added bonus. We agreed that to pack up lock, stock and barrel would have been audacious, so a three-month contract was negotiated, which would allow me to test the waters. I was cautious about making such a hasty decision when I had not yet worked for the company or lived in San Francisco (although I had visited in 1976). I also knew that you couldn't just pack up and move to a country without the correct visas in place. They did not seem too deterred by this, they just wanted me as soon as possible. It was such a boost to my ego to be offered a job overseas. In America to boot!

My kids were elated, my ex-husband was slightly bewildered that I could achieve all this without him, my friends were plain envious, and Michael was obviously fearful about our future together.

***

There is an element of mystique that courses through our everyday lives. Most of us simply choose to ignore it and therefore become bound to the banality of routine. I fervently adhere to the mystique, which seems to carry me where I need to go, like a river of possibility always flowing alongside us, invisible but perceptible all the same. In times of uncertainty, when the sublunary doesn't seem to answer my questions, I naturally source or find the appropriate people of this caliber to help me. This happened to me shortly before I left for San Francisco, and quite by accident. Or was it divine intervention trying to tell me something?

Sacrifice

I was on my usual Saturday morning jaunt to the supermarket. I always strolled through the local Orange Lane Markets on the way, which is a relic of the sixties, with artists and crafts people selling their wares, masseurs and mystics offering their unique personalized services to the public. I enjoyed the markets; they were a reminder of how simple life used to be, and it was often humbling to see that a lot of the crafts people actually made their living this way. On this particular day there was a mysterious Indian man with a long beard and turban, meditating outside his stall, oblivious to the noise and commotion happening around him. The signs on his stall indicated that he performed past life regressions with the help of angels. How interesting, how fascinating, how absolutely divine. I was hooked and the need to have a past life regression session with the Indian guru took hold! Having always been so curious about reincarnation I thought that perhaps he could clarify my feeling that Michael and I were living out some deep karmic drama.

I sat down directly in front of him and waited patiently. He appeared to be in some sort of trance, and I wondered whether he could feel my presence. Some 20 minutes later, he came to and proceeded to talk with me. I asked only about Michael and me and the possibility of lives we'd lived before.

It transpired (according to the Indian guru) that we had spent eight lifetimes together as unified male and female counterparts. Most of these lives were in other galaxies and lived as astral beings; only three times had we lived on Earth. Fascinating! But the real thunderbolt hit me when he told me that our most recent life together was just two hundred years ago, here on earth. Michael had been an aristocratic person of great importance to the community and held in high esteem by his countrymen, somewhere in central Europe. I was his servant in this lifetime, and although we were not married it was a relationship of commitment nonetheless. We lived out our whole lives together under the same roof, and I even bore him a son, whom he apparently adored. When I asked if his wife then (who was apparently cold and unloving) was the same one he has today, the guru said, "Yes."

I sat in total disbelief at what he'd just said, for the life he'd just described was a replica of an extremely vivid dream I'd had upon arriving back from England. It was a comforting dream in light of how depressed I had felt, and it replayed time and again in my head like a recurring fantasy. In my dream/fantasy/vision, I even remembered the commitment of the relationship and the son we had, how we were powerless to change the sociological class structure, but accepted the situation and the open deceit with which the relationship was conducted, under the one roof, between the three of us. The Indian asked me if I wanted to know the basis of our relationship. I said, "Yes."

He shuffled the angel cards and laid them in front of him. The card I turned over was the Archangel St. Michael, the Angel of Love. "He needs you more than you need him, and more than you realize," he said.

"Then why am I going to San Francisco?" I asked.

"Because you are following your heart," he said with a gentle smile.

Over the next few weeks, and also upon my return from San Francisco, I looked for the Indian guru, but he never appeared at the markets again. This seemed to have been his only (cameo) appearance.

Sacrifice

14th April 1996
Dear Barbara,

It was a lovely surprise to get your phone call last night. It was a huge tonic to hear your voice and I could picture you sitting on your bed early on a Sunday morning wearing very little, so I was able to go to bed with even more vivid images of you and your delectable body, which, by the way, I proceeded to ravish with an intensity that would have surprised even you!

I fell asleep with a smile playing on my lips, happy in the knowledge that I was loved by someone so very special to me. The pain of separation is made less acute by this emotional feeling and expectation of great times ahead. I loved your description of the session with the card reader in the Orange Lane Markets. It sounded both fascinating and thought-provoking, and the fact that one of our lives together coincided so closely with your recent dream was all the more intriguing. It's a lovely thought that we have already experienced many lives together, both terrestrial and spiritual.

I wonder...maybe that's why I had such incredible feelings of assuredness, positiveness and ease when I met you. I know I have said this before, but I swear that the very first instant I saw and met you in your Adelaide office something intangible stirred in my subconscious.

When we corresponded by fax last April regarding the Bordeaux trip, and especially when I phoned you about it, I swear I was subconsciously, even consciously, feeling very excited in anticipation of fulfilling my desire to get to know you better. Then when I saw you sitting in the reception of the Timotel in Paris on June 18th, 1995, I know my heart leapt a bit.

Dear Barbara, maybe it was the past within me flickering in recognition of a soul with which I had been in love several times before. This was not a meeting, it was a reunion of two loves lost, now re-found, of souls that had passed into darkness, and which were now able to fuse together to produce a light that could show us the way out of darkness into the bright, clean air of love.

You are now my lady, and the love we share can be revived for all to see and envy. The task we have now is to ensure that our faith in the power of true love and the path of our positive destiny is never diminished, and that we keep believing that we can be together soon, somewhere, somehow. It is amazing what can be achieved by positive thoughts and will power. We must trust what our hearts are telling and willing us to do.

Sacrifice

All I can say is that despite the difficulties, the imponderables, the physical separation, all the things that are not yet fixed or known, despite all this, I love loving you. I love being loved by you. Nothing compares, or has ever compared. The all-consuming feelings I am experiencing on many levels of my consciousness are such fuel for my fractured soul.

They soothe, console, inspire, energize, explore, and stimulate my whole being. I adore it as much as I adore, admire and want you.

I love you Barbara, I want to be with you forever, until the next life, and then I'll be with you again.

Michael

I was not feeling the same connection with Michael since I had returned, and I felt that I owed him an explanation, at the very least, as to why I had chosen to go to San Francisco. His letters still spoke of his undying love for me, but I could not hide, nor should I, the fact I was questioning our relationship deeply. I considered just turning off the tap of words, knowing what a powerful component these were in our union. After all, this was the basis of our relationship; of letters and plumbing the depths of our souls. Perhaps we had exhausted our letter writing, knowing that the relationship was stuck at a stalemate. However I could make a move, and one based on what was right for me. I knew instinctively that the San Francisco gig was a way out, a gift of insight and that not going would be to fight the current of the river, by holding on...to what?

18th April 1996
Dear Michael,

First of all, I miss you. Secondly, I'm lonely and depressed, and third, I've come down with a flu and have been forced to stay in bed to recover from my symptoms. There does not seem to be any remedy for the first one...

I have to tell you however that part of this depressed feeling is undoubtedly in response to my higher self revealing the reality of it all. The peripheral aspects of a relationship; your family members feelings, i.e. your children and brothers and the impact that had on me. And the fact that we have only spent five weeks together on holiday, and therefore in a deliberate romance zone, makes me question our union. The fear of it all becoming complacent and ordinary when we are together permanently frightens me. The feeling of responsibility I have for your predicament and the pressures you are receiving don't help either. My head is a mess of conflicting thoughts and therefore my heart is saying, "Go to San Fran."

I do know one thing though, that I did enjoy being with you and only you. We didn't seem to need anyone else to stimulate situations (well, apart from Desireé). In fact, I felt quite uncomfortable during the few circumstances we were with others. This was all probably owing to this new identity I had enforced upon me...being the other woman! I'm so used to being just me that this was like a new set of rules I wasn't used to. I guess this all helps to clarify the situation, and paints a very clear case for a totally new life removed from all these pressures and rules for us both.

I so enjoyed our time together in France, particularly from an exploratory perspective. We explored new places and we explored our bodies and minds some more. I loved the games we played, Michael, the laughter and tears...I loved it all. There was one moment that will be unforgettable in my mind and that was in the hotel on the Rhône. What fun and sheer joy to forget who you are, to become someone else and to experience sex for all its raunchiness and sensuality with someone I trust and love so utterly. I wonder how often you will be calling her?

I know that maintaining a playful relation-ship takes effort and initiative, and I am prepared to commit myself to doing so with you. You seem to understand so many of my needs...they're not too different from your needs, I know.

My acceptance of the San Fran offer will be testing for us both, I know, but I need this time out to find out what I really want. I am trusting the Universe as I feel that it was meant to be. I will call you when I get there.

Barbara

Going to San Francisco turned out to be a deeply personal pilgrimage. It was like returning to the scene of the crime (my marriage) twenty years on. I was about to let go of my past in a way I probably wasn't quite ready for, even though I'd left the marriage two years previously. It took me by surprise, but I acknowledged it and treated it as the gift it was!

The last time I had been in San Francisco was precisely twenty years ago, with my ex-husband. We'd been married only six months and were living in LA. It was our first holiday since we'd arrived in the USA, and we'd driven north along the Pacific Coast Highway, in our white '64 Mustang with red leather seats, up to San Francisco, stopping along the way at the quaint seaside towns of San Luis Obispo, Santa Barbara, Carmel and Monterey. I was only eighteen years old, he was thirty, and we were very much in love with each other. We were such carefree spirits then, before children, mortgages and the trappings of the materialism marriage gathers.

Consequently, everywhere I went; Fisherman's Wharf, Ghirardelli, Lombard Street, Golden Gate Park, Sausalito, all reminded me of another time. But where was my young, captivating husband? Here I was, exactly twenty years later, doing it all for myself, by myself, locked in a time warp. Nothing had changed but me.

I found myself pondering my past, and him in particular. I sometimes thought that had my husband been more understanding about my need for personal enlightenment, he would have let me go instead of holding on as tightly as he did. But the simple fact was, we were different people with new directions. He had adhered to the rule book faithfully, and by every measure he was a model husband. We looked the perfect couple, and when we had met twenty years prior, our agendas were in sync. He

Sacrifice

was twelve years my senior, but I looked older than my eighteen years, as young women sometimes do. Emotionally we both seemed equally ready for marriage. I had been brought up to expect nothing more or less from life than marriage and children. I was a woman and that was going to be my lot.

It was only some twelve years later that I began to wake up to a lot of things, mainly myself, rather than live up to others' expectations of who or what I should be. But it took eight years to leave, through the process of trying to deny it, do the right thing for everyone else, run from the shame of failure and the hurt I would inflict by destroying my little family of four. I wished my ex-husband could have heard my inner agony, but he refused to see or hear it, and therefore we grew apart, and the inevitable power battle began. Though we wouldn't have been the first couple this had ever happened to, I really had believed in the happy-ever-after endings. The only problem was, I had become desperately unhappy.

Perhaps marriage as an institution needs a readjustment. Forty or sixty years is a long time to live with someone, let alone guarantee that you will not change. Look at any couple twenty years after the 'I do' stage, and anyone can see that both have changed, at least physically. Many men have no hair and have grown a belly; some women lose their identity and confidence through tending everyone else's requirements.

Actually, on reflection, we were a couple that did not fit this mould. He still had all his hair, and looked remarkably good at fifty, and I had a blossoming career, which had somehow taken over my role as full-time mother and given me a new sense of identity along with buckets of confidence.

Perhaps with a different mindset at the time, I could have realized the perennial nature of our love, and he might have developed new dimensions, too. Perhaps, perhaps, perhaps! There are always so many roads that present themselves and we continually find ourselves at crossroads. It's not always easy to go back, and sometimes it's just too darned difficult to even make a decision.

After our San Francisco visit back in 1976, we'd travelled on to Yosemite National Park to camp with the bears, then over the mountains into the Mohave Desert. These were such exciting times for us, and such a brilliant way to start our marriage. Discovering each other in a new country was just an added bonus to the whole experience. I remember well the drive through the Mohave desert, all the way back to Los Angeles, on roads so straight we wound the Mustang up to 100 mph, singing loudly along to Mary Hopkin on the radio, "Those were the days my friend, we thought they'd never end..."

The day-long drive through the vast desert eventually led us to the descent into Los Angeles, with its sprinkling of city fairy lights at dusk fading into the horizon and merging into the pink-brown hues of smog that lay heavily over the San Fernando Valley. It was a majestic sight to behold, but a far cry from San Francisco. We'd both identified with San Fran being a sister city to Sydney, and wished we'd chosen it as our temporary home over LA. It was not possible for work reasons, but it became our favorite holiday destination during our two years in the USA, as it was just a day's beautiful drive up the coast to get there, and we could always roar back home on ramrod-straight Interstate 5 if we were pressed for time.

The memories flooded over me in waves as I recalled my time here with him. In San Francisco, it seemed like every corner and every turn held a reminder of my life gone by. In truth, San Francisco in 1996 became a grieving place for me to address

Sacrifice

the sadness of the end of my marriage. I had stayed so strong in order to move on and out of the marriage, and in the process I realized that I hadn't sat down and had a good old cry...for all the good times. Many times during the first month I would find myself poignantly reminded of our happy times together. It did not confuse me about my decision to leave, for I had made that decision with conviction, but when a melancholic moment grasped me, I'd cherish it, then let it wash away with the tears it produced.

For some strange reason I didn't feel the need to intimate this to my ex-husband, though he must have been having his own melancholic reflections on our early years together in the USA, as he wrote and gave me this beautiful and touching poem before I left. Perhaps this was why I was reflecting so much on my time there with him, all those years ago.

Poem for Barbara

Remember
Twenty years ago, Memorial Day
We visited San Francisco Bay

Remember...
that time and place,
Golden Gate, Fisherman's
Ghirardelli and Lombard,
so much come to mind.

Remember...
Good times between,
so fast they slipped away.

Remember…
We beautiful two,
Made into four.
Such beautiful boys,
now near men.

Remember…
So many roads to choose,
so much of life ahead.
We started out walking…
Now life has just begun, again.

Remember…
Love, light, harmony,
peace and happiness.
I wish them all
For you

Robert

I did however want to share the San Francisco adventure with my sons. They were only just beginning to realize the reasons why I'd left—my need for individualism without the confines of wife and mother roles. I was always conscious of the betrayal they must have felt by my leaving, and God only knows how guilty I felt. It was the highest hurdle, and the hardest thing I had ever done in my whole life—to leave my children after dispelling the discouraging myth that a woman should always put her children before her own personal happiness. In my heart I knew I had not left them. I always knew they would come back to me,

Sacrifice

on my terms, as a person who had her own aspirations, dreams and goals, not the doormat I had become in a family where we all lived out our roles in dissipated anxiety, resenting each other for what we weren't, or wanted to be.

San Francisco served as a bridge for us to communicate our bond in a new and unique way. I wanted to share it all with them as much as I could through letters and phone calls. The physical separation also helped, I'm sure, to give them a more appreciative insight to our relationship. Although they did not live with me in Adelaide, I was always there for them when they needed relief from their father, and they could stay with me whenever they wanted. Now, they seemed to be missing my being there for them. I found myself writing to them instead of Michael. It just felt right. I gave in to a lot of feelings that just felt right after experiencing my personal overview of going with the flow and feeling the cathartic process of sorting out my past.

When I lived in the United States twenty years ago, the agenda had been somewhat different. Our intention was never to remain permanently, but to make some easy money as a kick-start for our future, and to see some of America. Though by the time we left, had become very attached to the lifestyle and easy money. When you are younger, perhaps the environmental and sociological changes are easier to adjust to, but now I found myself (at thirty-eight) not attracted to the things I was at eighteen. I guess for a start I felt I'd been through it all before, which annulled the need to experience America first hand. Although there may not have been a lot of superficial difference between America and Australia, underneath the surface there was. Externally (to its detriment) San Francisco had not changed in twenty years, Fisherman's Wharf looked tired and in dire need of a makeover. Sausalito, the so-called artists colony with its cute artsy novelty shops, was past its use-by date. The majority of restaurants were still decked out with dark oak paneled walls, red and white checked tablecloths, and the menus were repetitive and predictable. These had not changed much in twenty years either.

I absolutely yearned for a proper Caesar salad, with a soft-boiled egg dripping over the lettuce, crisp pan-fired pancetta, maybe some anchovies tossed in for good measure with large pencil shavings of parmesan cheese. Not the shredded lettuce with grated Parmesan I always received. I was even served one once without any dressing. Now that was really something in the land notorious for it's mayonnaise!

On my weekend outings I'd always search for an alfresco café with umbrellas on a sidewalk, but do you think I could find one? They were as rare as anchovies in a Caesar salad. The norm was plastic chairs, plastic plates, polystyrene cups and plastic knives and forks. Everything in this land was all so disposable, giving the distinct impression of a flimsy cardboard society, ready to collapse with the next steady gust of wind.

I couldn't get into America because I couldn't find it. This great land of technological advancement, leadership and consumerism lacked soul. I felt the tendrils of a society in decay. A land of *'haves'* and *'have-nots.'* On every corner sat a beggar, if not two or three. The *'haves'* chose to completely ignore the *'have-nots'* as if they were lowly pigeons or worse, pieces of litter. I gave regularly to the beggars, particularly the ones who approached me. They would only ask for a quarter. When I gave them a dollar it became quite apparent that they did not receive this sort of generosity often. It was almost a shaming experience to say the least, because giving a measly dollar did not make me feel terribly generous in light of their situation. But it was the

Sacrifice

plight of their desperate situation that touched me so deeply.

These folk were ordinary people, sometimes women as young as thirty, with signs propped at their feet reading: *"Please help, eight-year-old son to support."* Often the men had signs hung around their necks made crudely from cardboard and rope, which read :*"Vietnam Veteran,"* this seemed to explain their plight in two simple words! It didn't matter what the reasons were, whether they were drug addicts and had brought their doom upon themselves, deserted wives, alcoholics, or war heroes, they seemed to me victims of a rapidly decaying society that no one wanted to claim responsibility for. They were ignored by the masses as surely as the litter and grime they lived among. Where was the dignity and justice for these poor folk?

Had I not seen this twenty years ago, or were my baby eyes not yet open enough to see? Were there more beggars now than back then, or was I just too caught up in my own Utopia, too blind to see the real world going on around me? When I enquired more about the plight of these poor souls, it got worse. These people were unemployable, therefore they were unable to contribute to a social security pension plan and could therefore never expect to receive a humble pension in their old age. Not that many of them would ever expect or probably even want to reach a ripe old age. There were not enough shelters for these homeless people, no hot meals, no soft beds, and no kind words, so most were condemned to the streets. I found the most appalling aspect was that the American government seemed to be doing nothing about its homeless people. My token dollars, or other tourists sympathetic contributions, which fell into the hands of a lucky few, ultimately would not change their situations. Only the government could give dignity back to these people by helping them. America, the richest nation on Earth, but rich in what? In my view, it was certainly not compassion. Anyway, that was the soap box upon which I stood (and still stand).

***

Michael joined me in San Francisco for a weekend early in my stay. We'd arranged it before I left Australia. My feelings about seeing him were mixed with physical longing and reserve due to my doubts about our relationship. The day he arrived I'd moved into my apartment on Nob Hill. I was so full of my own excitement that I nearly forgot he was arriving, and that I would be meeting him in the evening for dinner. That morning I'd transferred from the hotel to an apartment on the corner of Jones and Sacramento streets, and found myself in the middle of a movie shoot. It was a classic car chase, complete with fake tram lines, and a scene with a fake tram being shot right outside my new abode.

I sat and watched in awe, but I was suitably more amused by the movie I was directing, aptly titled *"Owning My Own Life"*. That realization was so powerful; to finally feel in control of my own destiny, and the thought made me smile from the inside out.

Circumstances meant I could not meet Michael at the airport, so he made his own way to my apartment. I then arranged a tryst that evening directly after work, at a place called Johnny Denton's. We both thought it suitably amusing to go so far away to another continent for a long weekend, just three whole days! Two months had lapsed since I'd seen him last, but it felt like only last week. Was it the uneasy feelings of doubt I'd not been able to rid myself of that made the whole thing seem less dramatic, less longed-for? We both knew that San Francisco would be a testing ground for us, and this must have contributed to our feeling reserved, unsure, and therefore not terribly loving.

Sacrifice

The lack of affection was evident to me, and by Monday I was relieved the weekend had finished. I found it difficult to discuss matters in depth with him in person, yet we had both been able to bare our souls and innermost thoughts in letters.

Michael lived with the fear that I would remain in the States if I chose to work with the American firm, and I was probably subconsciously creating this as a wildcard in the relationship. I knew this would test our love and his resolve to be with me. He'd declared it was me he wanted to be with, no matter where, but I knew he abhorred all things American and could never live here. Hypothetically, I knew this would never be, and so did he, but we never really got around to discussing it, even though we held fairly similar views. By Monday morning I really needed to air my feelings. We lay silently in bed, both awake but dozing as the morning sun rose over San Francisco Bay and lit the apartment. I yearned for him to reach for me, to take my sleepy relaxed body and arouse me awake the way he used to. Not able to tolerate this stand-off anymore, I got up, showered, and dressed.

He was surprised, and said, "I thought you were coming back to bed."

"Why Michael? Nothing was happening, and besides I have to go to work".

"I thought you were asleep." This was a lie, and we both knew it. He had been waiting for the right signal from me.

"Michael, I feel as though I am orchestrating your life, and I don't want to do that. I'll see you for lunch before your flight back," was all I could think of to say as I walked out the door. But at least it would give him an indication of how I was feeling, and perhaps give him the impetus to talk it through over lunch.

We never got to that stage however, for our lunch turned out to be a quick feed and a lovemaking session back at the apartment before his rapid departure. I was so touched at his gesture to make lunch and the intimacy of a nooner that the gnawing problems I'd wanted to address got swiftly swept aside. But they didn't go away, even after he did.

The airfare from England to America was nowhere near as exorbitant as to Australia, so we agreed that he would come out to visit once more before I returned in seven weeks time.

***

The company I was consulting to was a huge disappointment, perhaps possibly because I'd painted a different picture in my head. After working as a consultant on my own for six years, I was relishing the prospect of being involved with other designers and not having to deal with the business administration and print runs. I was incredibly nervous on my first day: the cab was late, and I hated being late; I couldn't decide what to wear, but eventually threw on a suit after experimenting with the entire contents in my suitcase, only to find that Californians dress down for comfort at work. My boss was a woman, and I found her sitting at her desk in bicycle shorts, a sloppy T-shirt, and sneakers. I politely asked whether she jogged to work, but she simply replied, "Oh God, no! I just don't have any client meetings today."

The rest of the office attire was pretty much the same, flip-flops, jeans, shorts, in fact I could have rocked up in a ballerina tutu or a Greek toga and nobody would have batted an eyelid. This was California!

My office consisted of a brick-walled room with the proportions of a closet, and through the window a view of another brick wall. My heart sank when I saw it, and I felt immediately claustrophobic being in it. It felt more like a cell than a room,

Sacrifice

and all the other designers were closeted away in their own cells with professional interaction between them on a need-to-know basis only. I tried my best to rearrange and sort through the piles of the previous designer's crap, but it seemed a futile exercise when the room was so small.

In frustration, I stacked it all behind the door and started from scratch with new utensils. The space could not be avoided though, and I continually bumped into the corner of the drawing desk when exiting the room, thereby developing a lovely bruise on my left hip. I noticed there was a spare desk in the production artists studio, which had a simple half wall between the hallway and the window to let light in. I eventually (and conveniently) moved myself there and claimed the spare desk as my own. The space was the only one with a half reasonable view (over a restaurant courtyard) and an ivy covered wall (ahh nature, lovely) and there was also a human being to talk with. Needless to say, we became good friends. She became my fondest memory of the company and my time there.

Unfortunately, there was no collaboration of creative ideas among the designers, as I'd hoped for. The work ethic lacked any sort of challenge and their design philosophy differed from my own; feeling that the clients needs were not addressed on an individual, abstract basis, which was how I worked. I was coming to realize that once you remove yourself from the employment market and work for yourself, you are effectively terminating that status and become permanently redundant from the work force.

The woman who owned and ran the business was not a designer. She had more of a passion for windsurfing than design, and spent more time under the Golden Gate Bridge than she did in the boardroom. I'd recall meetings in her office during which she'd gaze out the window and comment that the wind was up, then disappear for the rest of the afternoon and return at 6pm, windswept and salty. I secretly admired her attitude, but was still quite baffled at how she had built the company with such a laid-back approach. It didn't matter that the job was not up to my expectations, for it became a means to an end, a working holiday and the chance to review a lot of personal details. In fact, it was probably just as well for it immediately discounted the possibility of returning to the USA for work and one less thing I had to consider for my future.

The loneliness I had begun to experience became more acute by the fact that I was deliberately isolating myself from Michael and wallowing in memories of the past. I had been here for a month and a half, the halfway mark. It was time to move on and start having some fun. I needed a distraction and wanted to share the San Francisco experience with someone. So, when my employers took me and another designer out for dinner and to a club afterwards, I took full advantage of the opportunity. I was not going to let this chance slip by. It was my first evening out in four weeks (apart from when Michael was here). I don't know why, but I've never been able to go to clubs or bars on my own, possibly because perching on a bar stool looking like a piece of merchandise does not rate high on my list of favorite things to do. However, I also can't say that you meet the wrong sort of people in bars, for a wine bar was where I met my ex-husband. The chance of a romantic liaison in San Francisco was also greatly reduced by the fact that one third of the male population was gay.

At the club, after dinner, I worked the room and noticed a man staring right at me. Our eyes met and locked in a gaze of mutual interest. I walked by him, looking directly at him, bought myself a drink, and walked his way again. His stare continued

Sacrifice

as I stood there listening to the god-awful-head-banging music, pretending to enjoy myself.

He'll be here in a minute, I thought, and diverted my attention to the stage. I waited out the entire song, shooting a few quick sidelong glances in his direction. He was still staring. I'd never done this before. It felt natural, but perhaps I was doing something wrong. Eventually I decided that he must be just plain shy, so I walked straight up to him and asked if he was here alone.

"No, I'm with my friend Tom." (I really know how to pick 'em!) But having initiated the contact, and to cover my embarrassment, I asked if he and Tom would like to join my friends, and they did. Clubs are also futile places to meet people as you can't understand what the other person is really saying. You leave with no comprehension of the conversation that took place, it all being a melange of garbled messages and head nods, and if you're really lucky a few seductive looks.

But the following day he called and asked me out for dinner, confirming that he was not gay, I guess. I was excited about having a date, and getting to know an American man. The possibility of something developing to take away the loneliness was also appealing. Strangely enough, I did not feel as though I was cheating on Michael, even though our relationship was deeply committed. I wanted to test my own feelings again, and the very fact that I was excited at the prospect of going out with another man said a lot already.

As I sat gazing out of my apartment window waiting for him to arrive, a metallic blue Porsche came to a stop outside and I could see the man through the sunroof dialing on his car phone.

Sure enough mine rang also. "Hi, it's Roger. I'm here," he said.

I rushed downstairs and eagerly jumped into his car,

subconsciously thinking that it would have been nice if he'd come to my door and even nicer if he'd at least got out of the car to open my side. I was used to Michael's gentlemanly manners, but I pushed that thought aside with, *"When in America..."*

Roger lived on Russian Hill, which was the neighboring area to where I lived in Nob Hill. He'd chosen a restaurant close by, so close in fact that he had to park in his own garage, as finding a spot on the streets of San Francisco was like winning a lottery (apparently). But how convenient for afterwards!

He was a lawyer with his own practice, four years my junior, tall, dark, and wore glasses, he reminded me physically very much of my ex-husband. How ironic! It turned out the reason he had been staring my way at the club but did not want to approach me was because he suspected I was a spy, and could have been working for the firm he was currently suing! I thought. We talked a lot, as one does on first dates, about backgrounds and our respective jobs, but I wasn't feeling any attraction what-so-ever to him.

We walked back to his apartment. I wanted to be driven home, but he asked me in, and believing you can tell a lot about a person by the appearance of their abode, I became curious. It wasn't good. The first thing that failed to impress me was the home entertainment system, one that took up the entire wall, all contained in an enormous black box with doors which were supposed to cleverly conceal it. He was a closet couch potato! After the grand tour of the apartment and a peek in the fridge (no food), I had a pretty clear picture in my mind of the lifestyle he led. He hadn't offered me a drink because he didn't have any, but I had spied a bottle of white wine on the dining cabinet and politely asked if I could have some.

"Oh, I don't want to open that, it might be very expensive.

Sacrifice

Not that you're not worth it, of course." *Worth what?* I wondered.

The evening didn't really get any better from there on. He lit up a joint (as everyone in California seemed to do), which seemed to relax him sufficiently enough to cause a retreat to his bedroom. From the prostrate position on his bed he asked me to join him. I refused and wandered into the kitchen, taking up a post at the window where I could observe the hillside of houses, which all had goings-on inside. I found it intriguing to observe the people in their houses, giving insight to a typical Friday evening on a San Francisco hilltop. It was congested living compared to what I was used to. Some of the small houses had equally small back yards, but the owners had sanctified the spaces by creating beautiful gardens in their inner city living. I sat there for quite some time, witnessing the intimate *goings on* of others, prying voyeuristically into their lives through the exposed windows.

As I watched the assorted soap operas before me, I also began pondering over Michael and the stoned contrast lying in the bedroom. Theoretically I should be attracted to a tall dark handsome lawyer who drives a Porsche, but he'd had a complete personality triple bypass. He was also very rude and arrogant, which counteracted everything he did have going for him. I eventually went and stood in his bedroom doorway and asked once more if I could be driven home. He pleaded with me to join him on his bed, just for ten minutes, and just for a cuddle. When I refused, he also refused to drive me home.

"Fine, I'll walk," I replied, and left.

He called the following morning, very apologetic, asking if I made it home okay, but also to ask me out again. I don't know why I accepted, but could only put it down to loneliness, or was it sheer boredom? I think if I had been in my usual environment I would not have given him the time of day after that first date, but I kept giving him the benefit of the doubt and it never got any better. In fact it got worse. But he *'beat a blank'* and it was amusing, to say the least, finding out what made at least this male American psyche tick. He was used to women seeing him as a trophy, the ultimate marriage prize in the game of life. From our conversations I gathered that they wooed him, offering fabulous blow jobs and organizing his social calendar, and he simply went with the flow until he became bored with them. He was a bit bewildered that I wasn't offering any of this and I did not seem to want any of the pie either. I came from another country, which in his eyes probably accounted for my indifference.

Men and women in America seemed to be at war with each other. The battle of the sexes was far from over. I felt their whole society was suffering from a backlash reaction to feminism. Men wanted women back in the kitchen, and women were using this against them, when it conveniently suited them. The courtship ritual was still based on how much money a man was prepared to spend to impress his object of desire. A man's attractiveness was gauged on financial and vocational status.

When I'd told the girls at work that I was dating a lawyer with a Porsche (I should have elaborated that he was also a tight arse, egotistic and arrogant prick) they thought I had hit the jackpot. My boss also started rubbing her hands together, thinking that I would be staying around.

One of Roger's friends later revealed to me that he was tired of all the game-playing involved with the courtship process, and the money it was costing him. He'd consequently resorted to prostitutes, because it was easier to get laid and a darned sight cheaper. I didn't have the heart to tell him that it was probably the way he looked. They both thought it quite incredible that I actually wanted to pay my own way. I bought them both breakfast that morning.

It was as if American women had taken two steps forward and one step back. They wanted equality, but clung to old-fashioned values and applied rules and conditions to relationships, which in turn affected men's attitudes, creating the battle that raged between the sexes.

A few weeks earlier, I had met a man in the street while earnestly studying my tourist map. He'd asked me if I needed help (must remember that one for next time). He pointed me in the right direction, then asked me if I wanted to have a drink. There was a great bar on the pier that I'd always wanted to go to, so I accepted. It was a lively place with a beer garden outside, and it was the closest thing around to an Aussie pub.

If ever a magnet were to attract someone, he was the right one to air my views on America's decaying society, for he felt exactly the same way. We talked for hours over a few gin and tonics and beers. We'd enjoyed the afternoon's reverie and so continued on at Chrissy Fields under the Golden Gate Bridge with a bottle of wine.

We got on to the topic of men and women. He revealed to me he hadn't had a girlfriend in fifteen years because he doesn't have the right job or drive the right car, and yet he was very handsome. He did call, and even though I enjoyed his company on that one day, I never saw him again. Maybe my subconscious was telling me that this person wanted to have a serious relationship, which was dangerous territory for me right now. Perhaps I would have proven him wrong about women, but I never saw him again. One night of intellectual conversation, was all we were meant to be.

***

Michael was due to come out again in two weeks, and the whole prospect filled me with dread. I certainly hadn't fallen for Roger the Dodger, and I still cared deeply for Michael. But I was deliberately shutting Michael out in order to walk my own path for a while. It would be detrimental if he did come over for another visit, that I did know.

I called him that evening and woke him; it was very early morning in London. He sounded gorgeous, sleepy and sexy, and I almost faltered. I very nearly said, "Oh, I just needed to hear your voice," as we both had done on countless other occasions. But I mustered my steely resolve and told him that I didn't want him to come out because I was having second thoughts about a committed relationship, and certainly that I was not ready for living together (which was assumed by him) after knowing each other such a relatively short time.

I related how the past five weeks had brought about a realization that I wanted to experience and give more to my children, and I even told him I had started seeing someone. It came out in an effusion of cold, matter-of-fact, this-is-how-it-is dialogue, which left a stunned silence at the other end, so silent I could hear his pain. I said I was sorry, but knew how pitiful and inadequate my apology was.

My release from the impending visit, and the unburdening of thoughts I'd been carrying, gave way to a more carefree attitude with Roger. We hadn't slept together yet. I hadn't wanted to. But one evening after we'd been to see the movie *Mission Impossible*, as the credits rolled up, I turned to him and casually said, "Do you want to go to bed?" Naturally, he didn't object, but after his initial cries of, "Oh yes, oh yes, oh yes," I rolled over and thought to myself, *Oh no!*

I left his bed and walked home again. He was as uninter-

Sacrifice

esting in bed as he was out of it, or perhaps it was the blatant fact that nothing flowed between us that night, or ever would, but his semen. And it seemed I still hadn't earned the points needed to get a lift home.

I called Michael as soon as I got through the door, and pleaded with him to still come. Suddenly I was desperate for love, the real thing, and to be told I was loved and cherished by him. I wanted to sort out where we were in the relationship. I knew we were both carrying baggage from our marriages, and that the little quirks and games we had been playing smacked of past conditioning with our respective spouses. We both needed to dump our baggage at the *'lost property'* never to be collected again.

June 5th 1996
My Dear Barbara,

The past two days have been the most agonizing that I can remember, and I feel my head and my heart spinning like a satellite pitched out of orbit. To be awakened by your sweet voice yesterday morning was a pleasant surprise but it soon became apparent that what you had to say was going to have a profound effect on our relationship.

While I have always admired and respected your honesty, your directness of tone and unambiguous description of how your feelings and desires had changed came as quite a shock. It was not just that you had met Roger and had seen him and enjoyed his company and attentions in the past few days, it was also your telling me that you were no longer seeking a committed relationship with me in San Francisco or Adelaide or wherever. Also that you were finding it immensely difficult to sustain the relationship when time and distance so cruelly worked against us. You seemed so unequivocally certain that it would be wrong if I came to San Francisco, for both our sakes. The message was clear, so with a heavy heart I sent my ticket back, and pondered what all this meant.

Your call this morning fueled the cauldron of confusion that rages in my head. Your voice no longer had the hard edge of decisive thought and purpose, but the soft, vulnerable plea of a soul in a similar state of mental torment, a place where love and practicality fail to grasp each other's hands.

It was as if the previous day's conversation had never taken place. You rang at 8:30am. and it is now 10:30pm., and the day has been like hell on Earth. No sooner had I rung off when many of the mundane problems of life in the office relentlessly arrived in the form of phone calls, faxes and meetings. Then I had to rush to London for a crunch meeting with a client about prices. The traffic was

Sacrifice

fucking awful, the day hot, hot, hot...more traffic on the way home, then a promised supper with the children, both in the middle of exams. The end result was that it is only really now, some fourteen hours after your call, that I am able to attempt to piece together the events of the last forty-eight hours and what it all means.

All this during a day that, at every turn, pitched my mind back to nearly a year ago. The sun was shining, the car roof and windows were open, the fields green—just like last summer when my head spun with the discovery of a deep and meaningful love. I passed the shop in Putney where I bought the picnic before picking you up to go to Henley. Yesterday I was at Ransome's Dock. Barbara, I feared that this letter would be a jumble of thoughts. I dare not read it back for fear that it will seem a mess and I may tear it up! So forgive me, anyway.

What I need to say is that I too find the frustrations and difficulties of sustaining the relationship when physically apart for so very long, arduous. And I do fully understand how you must feel, and how difficult it is for you at the moment not knowing whether to make your mark in San Francisco, or return to Adelaide. Your most recent letter seemed to indicate that Australia was by far the most likely option. Though now it appears you may be having second thoughts. It is vitally important that you consider what is best for you and the boys—that's for sure. And if a committed relationship or the prospect of one fills you with alarm, then it is best that these feelings are fully aired now.

I would be a liar if I said to you now that I know exactly what I want. Rather, like you, the reality is that the dream often seems too much like a dream, with practicality breaking the spell with monotonous regularity. Even if employment in Australia (or the USA for that matter) were to be secured at a moment's notice, which is extremely unlikely, I doubt that I am ready to leave these shores just yet. There is much to consider, with the prime consideration being the welfare and well-being of my children. So it is unlikely that the relationship could struggle free from the bonds of physical separation for quite a while more. Can our souls bear that? Your desire, if we were to be together, that you would not like us to be living together, is one that I have difficulty in understanding right now.

If I were to be honest, part of the dream that has sustained me through these past eleven eventful yet frustrating months has been the vision of our lives fully entwined, woven with love and a yearning to explore each other. The love would be about sharing ourselves with each other—not others. And a mutual respect and lack of the mundane would prevent the need to glance over shoulders at greener pastures.

Dear Barbara, it pains me greatly to say this, but I feel it would not be a good idea if I came over on the 14th, and in any case I have returned

Sacrifice

the ticket. I fear that it might confuse you more if I came. Perhaps you need to be able to pursue your favored course, for you and your boys, without the burden of considering 'us'. You must follow your heart and happiness and fulfillment will surely follow. Whether that happiness involves me playing a key part in your life, I guess time will tell.

You thought the San Francisco adventure would be an important test for many aspects of your emotional and professional life, and so it is proving to be.

I recall when you told me about it. Half of me was happy and pleased for you, and the other half feared that somehow the spell might break. Something inside me wailed, "No, please don't go," but I had no right to say it, of course. Back in June, last year, something in the deep recesses of my soul was touched by the warm embrace of your being. No matter what happens, I know that the love that has gripped and enthralled me is real and rare, and cannot be forgotten. It will serve as a beacon of light should the night's darkness close in, or the tempest whip up the seas.

I do understand that you have to decide what is best for you, and how your life and your soul can be fulfilled, and how you can be reunited with your boys, how your professional life can be exploited to the full, how your physical needs can be satisfied and how your emotional desires can be met, cherished and developed. I sense that this is best done without considering the burden of me.

I too have to be clear how my needs can be satisfied, what I want, where I want to live, where I would work, how I would sustain the love of my children and my responsibility to them. Life in emotional 'purgatory' is difficult!

The path to true happiness seems to wind a torturous route with many hazards and pitfalls. I hope you discover the way to navigate the obstacles so that you find where the path leads. I'm here if you need me, my darling.

All my love,
Michael

Well, he had somehow let me off the hook, to enjoy the rest of my time in San Fran playing the field and finding my own way. But he always managed to leave the door open, just a smidgen.

***

I continued seeing Roger, and having unsatisfactory sex, though I found it quite intriguing to come across a man who didn't enjoy pleasuring a woman and was only interested in satisfying his own needs. The more I pushed him into sexual experimentation the more he backed off. We played out this power game, which was based on him having all the control. If I got my own way, whether it was actually being on top, or just going where I wanted to go for the afternoon, he felt as though he'd lost control and his mood would become irritable. Perhaps being a lawyer had something to do with it.

Sacrifice

We did have one interesting erotic experience, however. He'd called me around 3pm. and asked if I'd like to go for a flight in a small Cessna at dusk over San Francisco Bay. How could I refuse? His friend Charlie was a big time, big bucks lawyer who'd made a fortune and had his own plane. He regularly took it up over the bay to maintain his flying hours and impress his friends. Roger had told me that Charlie was a real playboy, and that I should watch out for him. Women apparently found him irresistible. It must have been the money because he was short, tubby, had terrible dress sense and was not what I'd exactly regard as playboy material. Still, that was just my subjective view.

As we strapped ourselves into the Cessna, Charlie turned around with a grin and said, "Don't do anything I wouldn't do."

'These boys with toys', I thought to myself. 'Well, I might as well have some fun if this is as good as it gets'.

After we'd passed over the San Francisco Bay and the pink dusk had turned to night, Roger and I slipped into the back seat and joined the *Mile High Club*. The erotic pleasure was gleaned entirely from doing it in full view of the pilot, with our clothes on of course.

Back on the ground, Roger strutted around like a dog who'd just discovered he can lick his own balls, while Charlie and I immediately opened and drank a bottle of wine. We chatted away about his sexual exploits. I was finding the American male to be a hugely entertaining species! The poor man was forty-five years old and had never come across one woman he ever wanted to be with for more than an hour. He saw women simply as conquests. There were so many and all so different, and there was so little time! He was the one who frequently visited prostitutes, which made me think he had a sex addiction. I felt sorry for him.

Charlie left Roger and me at a quaint Italian restaurant in the city. It was around 10:30pm., and because a lot of kitchens close up around that time, I'd checked in to see if they were still serving. The ambience was incredible, owing to the fact that the only lighting was candlelight, and it was occupied entirely by good-looking men. I must have had a disheveled sexual glow, because they all stopped and looked at me in awe as I spoke (or was it my accent?): "Are you still serving?"

And after a long pause, the owner finally replied, "Of course darling, I'll serve you."

I then realized it was a gay bar. But it didn't seem to matter, so I went to fetch Roger. We left the dinner selection to Ralph, the owner, as we didn't want to cause too much fuss at such a late hour. He cooked up the most wonderful plate of spaghetti with clams, tomato, and chilli for us to share, then proceeded to sit with us and chatted about everything from what nuns wear under their habits to the average rainfall in Tokyo. It would have been too bad if we had wanted an intimate dinner for two, because he just could not stop talking. Which was just as well, because even though the restaurant was exquisite, and the food sublime, I never felt any inclination to be the least bit romantic with Roger, nor did I expect it from him. But he managed in his usual style to spoil the whole evening by asking me for a *"contribution from my pocket."*

He had adjusted well to my equal standing when it came to paying my way, but I'd noticed that on the last few occasions I'd picked up the bill completely. And I guess I was starting to keep score, which was a very bad sign. I really don't know why, but I kept seeing him right up until I left San Francisco. On my own home soil I probably would not have, but I was fascinated by my feelings of eventual disgust for him and inwardly I picked him to

Sacrifice

bits as he revealed all his flaws.

He turned out to have all the traits I absolutely loathed in men. His car for one, even though the love of his life, revealed all his bad habits and the space at the rear was littered with McDonald's wrappers, Coke bottles, and beer cans, which I found absolutely disgusting and I told him so every time he collected me to go out. "Still haven't put the garbage out I see".

But I was in a new environment and no one knew me, so I found myself playing a part, sometimes being the kind of woman I thought he liked, then going back to the real me, which made him look closely at some of his actions. It was interesting to gauge his reactions, and I knew I was game-playing, but I didn't care. I wasn't hurting him in any way, just shaking up his corny ideals about women, which I thought he deserved. My last words to him upon parting and leaving the country "See ya Roger. No, maybe I won't. It was nice knowing you," and I felt like giving him a handshake rather than a kiss.

And the *only* letter I wrote to Michael during the whole three months I had been there confirmed that I still felt as I did before I left, with perhaps a little more clarity.

***

27th June 1996
Dear Michael,

As my assignment draws to a close, I find myself counting the days till I return. Two to go. Exactly this time last year I was in Taormina and you were calling me constantly whilst I sipped my G&T by the pool. What a contrast and what an eventful year it has been. I have made a clear decision on what the next stage is to be.

Coming to San Francisco, it has turned out, was not about job opportunities, or a lifestyle change. It was about letting go. It was a time of self-discovery, where I could be just me in an environment totally foreign and with no one else's judgment. Only I could make the decisions necessary for my future, and I needed to be totally free of any influencing factors in this process. Of course you know what I am talking about—us!

It has been 'time out' for me; away from everything. I got away from my kids, my business, my ex-husband, my friends, Felix the cat, my beloved Australia and Adelaide, and though you weren't physically in my life, it was time away from you, too.

Sacrifice

I had mentioned that when I first arrived in San Fran I was flooded with emotions of a love gone, my marriage, as if I'd stepped into a time warp from twenty years ago. My grief was powerful, and I cried a lot for the passing of my marriage. I realized that I had not acknowledged the end of my marriage when I had left, and found there was still a lot to be addressed. I simply went with the flow, and in time the feelings exited as rapidly as they'd entered.

The next emotional encounter was with my feelings of guilt for having left my sons. They both called me constantly to say they missed me, and were discovering their own feelings about me, in that even though I didn't live with them any more, it was still nice to have me just down the road. They probably feared that they might lose me on a more permanent basis if I came back to San Francisco to live.

I found myself wanting to share everything with them. Every time I got on a tram or had an 'American experience', I would find myself wishing I could recount it to them. Not even a trip to America for them would ever compensate for my leaving, and in my heart I knew this. I tried hard to like it here for that reason, to fit in and make it all work so that I could offer them an American experience in the future. They thought it was very cool to have their mother working in the USA. I addressed this by asking if I could be a cool mom in Australia instead, and said that I would not be doing them any favors by moving to America, even for a short term. There seems to have been a considerable gap bridged through my coming here, for which I am grateful.

The professional aspect was simply a walk down the employee path, and was probably the easiest to address. I knew after the first week that the company was not for me—or was it the other way around? Which leaves me finally with us. Oh God, where do I begin?

Last March, we experienced outside in-fluences on our relationship for the first time. I have very mixed feelings about our two weeks together. The time spent in the south of France was brilliant, followed by the week in London, during which time I was slowly introduced to your family along with their negativity towards me. These feelings haunted me for a long time. When I arrived back in Australia, I simply could not shake the feelings of despair I had. You were also a bit 'down' in your home territory, and I wondered whether that was your normal persona, and it scared me!

I came back to Australia feeling depressed and confused about us, so when this San Fran opportunity came up, I saw it as a chance to escape, I confess.

Perhaps both our souls would rather play than conform, though I am wary of a balance which needs to be struck, somehow. I found my-self questioning a lot of things in the following week, and I know you felt it, too.

Sacrifice

This made me quite scared of co-habiting with you without a suitable period of courtship, even though we had talked of it often. I would need a period during which all the little things get ironed out, somehow. When you get to say to me, "Hey, I don't like the way you molt like a cat all over the bathroom floor," and I get to say, "Well, fuck you, buddy!" or words to that effect.

It was all just sort of assumed that when you finally came out to Australia, we'd shack up together. I felt that there was such a big gap between holiday romance and permanency. If going to San Francisco seemed as though I was running away, I guess in truth I was, but it was a poor excuse and you deserved a more honest explanation before I left, rather than my sabotaging the relationship the way I did.

Going back to a year ago, I know that you were deeply inspired by our conversations of being honest in life during the journey to Bordeaux. I guess it is now time for us both to reflect on an eventful year. I do admire the courage it took to do what you knew was necessary, and if I sustained you through it then I have been of value to you and played my part.

But I sense, Michael, that without my con-stant love and urging, you have slipped back and lost that resolve to commit to a long-term relationship with me in Australia. Until you can break free of your own self-imposed constraints and rules, then you have nothing to offer me, except love via telepathy, fax, phone, letter, or email. We both know that it is not enough, don't we?

Halfway through this stint of self-discovery in San Fransisco, I gave up trying to make it all work: this place, the job, you and me. Then everything just started falling into place, as if a flow was happening, and I just went with it and started having fun. Every day felt like I was on a movie set in which I was the key actor, but deep down I knew I was also the director. San Francisco of course helped with the fabulous backdrop!

My friendship with Roger has been but a catalyst to realize I have needed a lot more from a relationship and I can't put my life on hold indefinitely for you, as much as I love you.

And so where to from here, you ask? I can't offer you any direction Michael. You must find it in your own heart and do what you feel is right for you.

With love,
Barbara

On my final Friday in San Francisco, I received a call from the boss at around 3pm ordering me down to Chrissy Fields, where all the windsurfers congregate under the Golden Gate Bridge. She also instructed me to put on something really cute! I was thirty-eight, and think I'd well and truly passed the cute stage of my life. But I didn't have a problem at all with leaving work at 3pm as instructed, and decided to take a leisurely walk back to my apartment through Chinatown instead of taking the cable car, contemplating what she might have in store for me. I slipped into

Sacrifice

jeans and a checked shirt, tied it at the front instead of tucked in (for the cute factor) then caught a cab down to the bridge.

I found her sitting in the back of a van in a wet suit, all salty and windswept as usual, with her two best friends, Dave and Hank. They were a couple of fifty year old surfers, long-haired, blond, bronzed and dressed in beach garb my kids would have worn. I was to find out later that they were indeed big kids who simply refused to grow up. Actually, I think I pretty well summed that up at first glance. They were all drinking vodka and cranberry juice from plastic hip flasks, and smoking weed. What a great way to finish the holiday, I thought, and got right into it. I felt very comfortable with them. They were a couple of cards, and thankfully there was no physical attraction, so I was able to completely be myself without the need to impress.

I thought it amusing that her best friends were a couple of guys, but it didn't totally surprise me, as it seemed that this woman regularly *'ran with the wolves'*. This was my last weekend in San Francisco, and now I was finally starting to feel some of its essence, or was it the marijuana?

My boss seemed to have the art of making things happen with as little effort as possible. She never forced things, and had time to do what she really wanted to, her passion - wind surfing! I watched the other windsurfers dart across the whitecaps under the bridge. It looked exhilarating. She'd told me that when her marriage fell apart, she wanted to get out there and compete with the boys. She'd surpassed most of them at the sport, acquiring their admiration and friendship along the way. To overcome her fear of *everything*, she'd bungee jumped from a hot air balloon.

"If I can do that, I can do anything," she said.

I don't know if it took bungee jumping to overcome trepidation, rather, perhaps a mindset of determination and focus. But I did admire her guts. I was suddenly looking forward to getting back to Australia, my business, and designing my own way again. The marijuana we'd smoked was having a profound effect on all of us. I quite often feel as though I am connected to other people and consequently pick up on their vibrations and thoughts. The weed was certainly accentuating that feeling between us.

We then proceeded to her fabulous multimillion dollar house in Sausalito. She had been entertaining house guests for the past two weeks, and at the first opportunity after their departure and her release as host, had headed for the bay. However, their flight had been delayed, so they were still unexpectedly and inconveniently present when we rolled up. Her guests were true conservatives from the East Coast: a college friend, her husband, and their eight-year-old son. I could see she had absolutely nothing in common with these people anymore, and how arduous the past fortnight must have been for her. So there we were, stoned to the eyeballs, trying to be incredibly polite and sober. Dave, Hank and I frequently lost it and would dash and hide somewhere, leaving her to handle it while we fell into uncontrollable fits of laughter. We'd compose ourselves temporarily, only to back off again into hiding somewhere in her conveniently large house.

Eventually the house guests left and the moment we'd cheerily waved them off, the music went on, the BBQ fired up, the red wine was opened, and the weed came out again.

Her house was stunning, contemporary in style, a typical southern California western red cedar split-level, with magnificent views over the Sausalito Marina. At every level was a deck, and on the ground level, a swimming pool heated to bathtub temperature. The barbecued salmon steaks with black rice and salad had been washed down by an obscene amount of wine, and now we were ready for a sobering swim.

Sacrifice

Before we plunged into the pool, I found my favorite *Enigma* CD in her collection, *The Cross of Change,* put it on and turned it up really loud. I'd never been so stoned or felt so good as I did floating in her pool, the music reaching deep inside, sending me crazy cosmic messages I already knew, but which needed to be reaffirmed. I felt at one with these friends and everything around me. I felt connected to everything: I was the liquid water I was floating in, the music was my beating heart, and the sparkling night sky—the roof over my head. This woman who had invited me to work for her was responsible for my coming to San Francisco, she had benefitted from my talent, but I didn't feel obliged to her in any way. She had offered me an opportunity, which only made me realize that I have it all already, even the tools to build a company such as hers.

I thought back to how my business began, which was quite accidental. I'd never intentionally chosen label design as a field to specialize in. The first label was so successful, I'd found myself with more commissions, and then it all started to snowball. It had all happened by the right people coming into my life at precisely the right moment, like magic. I'd managed to hold onto it all very tightly and neatly though, preferring to do everything myself, knowing that it was being done correctly. Over the past year or so I had been feeling the strain of it all, and my relationship with Michael was a welcome relief to my masculine working side always having center stage. I had drawn on my animus to leave my marriage, also. It had taken resolve and courage I didn't know I had. Michael had brought out my feminine side, and I'd given in to it quite willingly, but my business had suffered through my lack of attention to it.

And now, as I floated on my back in the warmth of the pool observing the universe, I reflected on my stay in San Francisco and what a marvelous journey it had been. I felt as though I had been through a cleansing and felt exuberant and full of energy to tackle the road ahead, and for once I could see around the corner with a clear full view. I needed to go home and get on with business, my business. It was the only thing right now that I could rely on, that was evident.

As the night's events drew to a close, I was offered a ride back into the city with Dave. After much insisting from my boss that I stay the night, I decided to take the ride as I did not want to face the indignity of being at my boss's house with the impending hangover I knew I'd have. I wanted the comfort of my own bed. How Dave managed to drive in the state that we were all in is beyond me.

Halfway over the Golden Gate Bridge we realized we were being stalked by a patrol car, possibly for driving too slowly. The siren went on, and we pulled over. Dave was asked to step out of the vehicle, which he did, and was questioned for what seemed to be forever. To this day I don't know why I did this, as it went against all reason. I could see them conversing through the rear vision mirror and they seemed to be having a pretty laid-back conversation. In my usual casual manner, I alighted from the van and joined in the conversation to try and move things along.

I failed miserably. They took one look at me, or was it a sniff?, then made the poor guy walk a straight line, which he couldn't do. They immediately slapped handcuffs on him and drove him away. Apparently his registration sticker had expired, and he had failed to put the new one on display. That's why they had pulled him over. I'm the one whose apparent drunkenness had made them think about alcohol being involved. Oops!

But now I was stranded halfway across the Golden Gate Bridge. The police officers could not arrest me, because I was not the driver of the vehicle. I was really annoyed that they had ruined a perfectly nice evening and arrested my cool driver. They had phoned for a cab, and while I was waiting for it to arrive, I stepped off the pavement onto the road, repeatedly, to pass the time. Then I heard a voice come over a loudspeaker: "Step off the road, and back onto the pavement!"

Far out. Where the hell did that come from? I thought.

So I stepped back up to the pavement, then back down to the road.

"Step off the road, and back onto the pavement!"

This was fun, so I played this little stepping onto-and-off-the-pavement game just to mess with the gatekeeper's head, and before I knew it, I saw more flashing lights in the distance—a patrol car speeding along towards me. Just in the nick of time, my taxi rolled up, and I jumped in.

"Step on it buddy, I'm in a hurry to get out of here," I said, thinking "How American can you get?"

I really was eager to get home to Adelaide and on with my life now. Dave's dog spent the night locked in the van without water. I spent most of the weekend nursing a hangover from hell and poor Dave spent the night in the clink with a bunch of desperadoes. It cost him $2,000 to raise bail!

***

Before I left, a card came from Michael saying he was off to Portugal with some friends for a week's holiday, which was the replacement trip for the time he had allocated to spend with me in San Francisco. Somehow I sensed he was going with a woman. I knew he was lying and it angered me. Or was I angry that he could move on so quickly considering the intensity of our relationship. I had also been quite stunned with his alacrity in cancelling the second trip to San Fran. I would rather have not received any correspondence at all, which only fueled my resolve to get on with my life without him, as he had without me.

***

It was somehow appropriate in a way that my ex-husband and the boys were there to greet me at Adelaide airport upon my return to Australia. I had a booty-load of stuff for them and they were excited about the snowboard and laptop computer, among other gifts I had bought them. They seemed genuinely pleased to see me, and because they'd cut their long hair they looked more like young men. Both boys looked a little older and even more handsome.

It had crossed my mind many times that they might want to live with me if I took up residency in the States, and I entertained the fantasy often. It was the only positive fuel I could have mustered as a reason to stay. God knows I had lots of Brownie points to make up, but at the end of the day, it was my life and I had to do what felt right for me. I had wanted to be able to make up in other ways for the family unit I was never able to complete. To open a door to the world for them, and offer experiences they could not have in Australia. Was that compensation for leaving them? Instead I could only share my San Fran adventure with them, and hope it would inspire them to have adventures of their own some day.

I seemed to have acquired a new perspective on a lot of things I had taken for granted before. Friends were one. I'd made so many good friends since I'd left the marriage, and I enjoyed cultivating the relationships. They were as important to me as

Sacrifice

my family. My small townhouse took on a special glow when I compared it to what I'd have to sacrifice it for had I chosen to live in San Francisco. I wouldn't be able to afford the standard of living I enjoyed in Adelaide. The best part about being back on Australian soil was the space, the accents, and the easy-going friendliness of its people. How I'd missed all that. Sometimes we need to go away, far from what we know and love to really appreciate what is already in our own back yard.

It was good to be home, Toto!

Rather than curse
our badly behaved lovers,
we grow to see those partners
who hurt us as true angels,
our nemesis or sacred enemy,
holding up a mirror for us.

Ruth Ostrow

CHAPTER 5

The final act

[AUSTRALIA - Adelaide - July / October 1996]

One of the last labels I designed before I went to San Francisco, was for Geoff Merrill, one of the more flamboyant and unconventional winemakers in South Australia. The name of the label - WHO CARES!

"You can't drink the label, so who cares what it looks like," he states. This was Geoff's way of thinking; he thought of it during a game of golf so he told me. Having successfully created Cockatoo Ridge (now sold for a handsome profit) he was now on to his next big wine venture. And I had conveniently arrived back in Oz just in time for the launch.

When a new wine brand is launched into the market it needs promotion. The best and most cost effective advert-isement is usually via wine writers (or critics, in which case the whole exercise can also backfire if they don't give the wine a favorable write-up). The wine writers are schmoozed and lubed fairly liberally and this usually takes place in a fancy restaurant where food is matched to the wine, which is the norm. Geoff always had a unique approach to his business ventures. The launch of Who Cares took place at Geoff's holiday home on remote Thistle Island, located smack bang in the middle of the Spencer Gulf, where the only access to the island is either by a two and a half hour ferry ride from Port Lincoln (an eight hour drive from Adelaide) or by private chartered flight. A Cessna was therefore chartered to fly the wine aficionados and supplies to the launch.

Thistle Island is remote. There are no shops, businesses, or basic amenities, not even a petrol station, so all living supplies must be transported with you on the day. There is no airport, just a dirt landing strip. Only two people inhabit the island full-time, along with some three-hundred sheep, and thirty-odd holiday homes, which are uninhabited most of the year.

Being the second largest island off the South Australian coast, second only to Kangaroo Island, it is also rich with wildlife and natural wonders such as saltwater rock pools and limestone caves, along with historical preserved ruins of early settlers. Some sixteen kilometers in length and only five kilometers wide, it covers an area of four thousand hectares. Beautiful pristine secluded beaches abound on the east coast of the island, contrasting dramatically with spectacular limestone cliffs and rocks which are battered constantly by the Great Southern Ocean on the west side.

***

The *WHO CARES* launch event was organized in conjunction with Geoff's distributor; we all met up at the distributor's premises to collect the day's supplies before piling into the minibus for the airport. Geoff was known for his antics in the wine industry and his unseasonable sense of humor had led him to make life-size cardboard stand-up figures of himself especially for trade shows, where he would place them behind the counter and then leave to do some serious networking. He would more than likely be found at the pub networking with the locals. Ironically, he was also a very good friend of Michael's, the two of them often caught up whenever they were on each other's turf.

We knew there would not be enough of Geoff to go around

Sacrifice

for all of us and so we loaded the cardboard Geoff and a cooler containing four dozen oysters on ice, some loaves of fresh crusty bread, cheese, a few cases of *WHO CARES*, and headed for the airport.

I sometimes wonder if it is other people's energy we tap into when we create our own natural endorphins, because this day was like no other and I will remember it as one of the best I have ever experienced.

On the tarmac preparing to board the plane, Dianna (his distributor) suggested a few publicity pictures. So we propped cardboard Geoff up by the plane, ready for the photo shoot, fighting over who was going to do the worst things to him for the photo. We were falling over ourselves in fits of laughter preparing for the raunchy photos with cardboard life-size Geoff, but the darned camera wouldn't work! The pilot silently observed the crew he had for the day, and must have decided that we were all either already drunk, or a bunch of loonies, but he quickly got with the programme and came to the rescue with his camera.

With the photo shoot complete, the pilot then summoned us all to the plane and looking directly at me, remarked, "and who wants to be my co-pilot?"

What could I say. but "YES, I'd love to!"

Wearing the all too serious headphones and being instructed on how to take off, brought me back to earth somewhat, until I realized that he was kidding and I didn't need to do a thing. We flew up the coastline from Adelaide, heading north, then veered off into the Gulf of St. Vincent over the Yorke Peninsula and then into the Spencer Gulf. It was amazing to look down on the landscape from the height we were at in the Cessna, probably a mile high. You could clearly distinguish all the elements of the landscape below. I saw all sorts of shapes: animals, fish, skeletons. It reminded me of the mysterious field patterns which occurred on the English landscape a few years back, supposedly created by aliens or some clever guy with a lawn mower. There were small forests of trees and bushes, all so perfectly laid out from our vantage point that it quite literally looked like an artists canvas.

"Hey, who's been drawing on the landscape?" I asked through my headphones.

He looked over and smiled.

"Who is the blonde?" he replied back.

Blondes win, every time, I thought. "Oh that's Dianna, yeah nice lady, real nice, you fancy her?"

"Well, yeah. I could"

"Leave it to me, I'll see what I can do."

"That would be good, she's chartering this flight, right?"

"Umm yeah, I thought you knew who was who here, and who was in charge? She's a bit ditzy," I added jokingly. "You know after all, she is a real blonde!"

He chuckled, then revealed that he'd had us on loud speaker! I turned around and they were all grinning at me. Dianna was not so amused, however!

We talked nonstop for the duration of the trip and had a good laugh about the black box being discovered if we crashed, and what they'd hear as we were *going down*!

Before we landed on the island, we flew around it a couple of times, getting lower and lower before approaching the dirt landing strip.

***

Sacrifice

Geoff and his family were there to greet us. What a welcome sight! His family (consisting of two young daughters under 10 and his wife) sitting atop of two old, beat-up Land Rovers, holding two *WHO CARES* banners, waving and singing wildly. I couldn't tell you what they were singing. It didn't sound in tune at all. It was the craziest brand launch I've ever been to. Whereas most launches can be so predictable, this was totally informal, just a tad wacko and therefore unexpected, surprising and thoroughly entertaining. I think the journalists thought it was a joke and were wondering when it was going to get serious, but I loved it for precisely what it was, nutty and nonsensical, but who cared!

However, this reminded me of how much I loved this carefree country and also the poignancy of what Michael loved about this breathtakingly beautiful land. Especially on a day like this, Australia at it's best; the stunning clear cyan skies with gods and angels adorning the stratosphere, smiling down on the earthlings at play. A place of non-conformity, where you can be yourself effortlessly and accepted for precisely who you are. Michael, being a friend of Geoff's also brought to fore the realization of another realm. Had our plans to be together gone smoothly then he would have most certainly been here with me at my side right now, enjoying this experience together.

The Land Rovers were incredibly uncomfortable. They had simple iron bench seats along the windows in the back, facing inwards. They reminded me of the hot air balloon trip with Michael last November. Was I ever going to get him out of my head? We piled in and began the bumpy ride along the dirt roads to one of the cliff tops high above the ocean, where we enjoyed the first tasting of the *WHO CARES* white wine. The hot rays of the sun danced across the ocean and we could see the schools of salmon jumping all at once out of the ocean. I was entranced by the view and could have stayed there all day, watching the ocean offer up its magnificent array of visual delights. This was Geoff's favorite contemplating spot. How lucky he was.

The journalists were finally starting to chill out. Or perhaps that long needed drink of white wine accompanied by tasty fresh South Australian oysters did the trick. From the cliffs, we then ventured to the other side of the island, which was bearing the full brunt of the ocean waves from the westerly swell. The waves were exceptionally large. We were fortunate to have such a show on a relatively calm and beautifully sunny day. We walked over the rocks to where the rock wallabies hung out. It was at this stage that I lost the bet that my white jeans would stay white all day. I slipped on some water and landed on my rear end. Of course they all accused me of having too much to drink, but in truth I was just in a hurry to see the gorgeous little creatures that were hopping over to meet us. The locals had managed to make friends with the wallabies by feeding them, which had consequently earned their trust.They voluntarily approached humans and expected a good feed, allowing us to pet them while we offered up bread and fruit. It was pure joy sitting there amongst my newly made friends, the rock wallabies, basking in the sunshine.

We reluctantly left our little friends all lined up, their dear little faces showing genuine disappointment that we were leaving so soon. Our last port-of-call was *'The Washing Machine'*, a huge hole in the rocks' surface where the ocean gets in but can't escape quickly enough. The frothy water was churning around very much like a washing machine, the forces of nature mesmerizing to watch. Many times during the day, while on the cliff top looking out at the powerful ocean, I was reminded of how the tides of life inevitably also ebb and flow, in and out, back and forth. Sometimes life, like the tides, is powerful and majestic, sometimes it is calm. It had been calm for quite some time in my life. I'd been wading around in the gentle waters, sure that something powerful was well overdue. Being in such close contact with nature is always balm for the soul and this was that at its very best.

The tour of the island now over, we relaxed over lunch at Geoff's house, continuing the tasting of the *WHO CARES* red wine. Of course nothing could surpass a good old Aussie BBQ and we expected nothing more (considering the theme). A Goanna lizard had made its way up onto the balcony while Geoff cooked, another hungry visitor wanting a handout. He was big and scary, so he did not get an affectionate pat from me, or anyone else for that matter. After a brief visit, he meandered over to the other side of the patio, down the stairs and off into the bush.

I didn't mind the wild animals at all. In fact I found them very safe and non-threatening. But when the pilot made a move on me and whispered in my ear, "I bet you've got nice, firm breasts," I totally lost my nerve and got scared. He brought me right back to earth. I really didn't want to be bothered with any sort of sexual antics, and felt that he'd stepped over the line of innocent flirting just a bit too far. So began the game of trying to put as much distance or people between him and me as I possibly could. We had all consumed a fair bit of wine by this stage, except the pilot of course, and I didn't appreciate him taking advantage of my relaxed state. His approach, inappropriate as it was, also made me think about Michael, and how I liked the safety of being in a relationship. Not that it would stop creeps from coming on to me, but it got me thinking all the same. Doesn't every woman want to be rescued by a man, that prince on a white charger? Rescued from herself and from situations like this? It's as if when in a committed relationship you get this *'taken'* stamp tattooed across your forehead, instead of the *'Yeah, I'm up for it any time, buddy'* note that someone has cruelly stuck to your back.

The day's events finally came to a close with the family bidding farewell to us at the landing strip, on top of their vehicles once more - waving wildy - probably glad to see the end of us in reality. Getting in and out of those Land Rovers, which didn't have steps, proved to be an exercise in extreme concentration. We each balanced on the tow bar before hitting the ground, some hitting quite literally. And needless to say I wasn't offering to be the co-pilot on the return journey. I sat in the back of the plane and reflected on my day.

I found myself wanting to share all of it, with Michael. I did care. I wanted him back. But there was no contact from him. Every day I awaited his call or a letter, but nothing came. It was the strangest feeling to be back in my home, which emanated so much about us. Since I had moved into my new townhouse immediately after my return from Bordeaux, all my memories were of times I'd experienced or shared with him. Even on my birthday dinner party, he'd called and been a part of it. My Saturday nights watching videos were comforted immensely by his phone calls. A satisfaction and contentment like that only comes from a deep love. My phantom lover had departed his haunt, and I missed him desperately.

I thought I could come back and just start my life afresh, but I craved his contact like a crack addict craves a fix. The following weekend I called him and asked how Portugal had gone. He said, "Fine."

I then asked if he had gone with a woman. There was silence. "Yes, I did," he replied.

Jealousy immediately coursed through me like a venom. I was annoyed that he had not volunteered the information, considering

Sacrifice

the honesty upon which our relationship had supposedly been based. It seemed quite clear that I was easily forgotten and that he had quickly and readily moved on.

My reaction prompted an explanation via a letter. I devoured the letter, relishing every word, and even had it for breakfast the next morning again.

July 16th 1996
My Dear Barbara,

I've just been reading through some of our old letters and faxes that have accumulated in the huge file over the past year. In some ways, last July seems only days away, at times it seems an age away. I came across a letter I wrote to you exactly one year ago, late at night on the eve of my birthday. I was alone in the kitchen, with my music, and the household asleep upstairs. Here I am, one year on, late into the evening whisky at hand, Enya on the CD, this time alone, in my own flat on the eve of my birthday again. Perhaps a time to reflect. So many of those special feelings that were awakened in me continue to flood over me, without perhaps the passionate intensity that characterized those early days.

But not withstanding that, the love I still feel for you is real and transcends much of the day-to-day problems that our separation and changing circumstances have caused. A brief look through the photo album, a glance through the pile of correspondence, or merely conjuring up your image, your voice, your body, and I feel your soul close to mine. It helps me to realize that there is a distinct part of my heart that holds you close, and always will, no matter what. It's very, very special, and I am more complete for having found your love.

The past few months have proven to be difficult times for us both. The frustration caused by the difficulty of maintaining and building upon the relationship, given the various circumstances which have conspired to weaken our resolve, have almost caused me to commit the cardinal sin of losing faith. Your move to San Francisco was a poignant reminder to me of how frail my resolve could become if I weren't careful. How relatively easily my bravery in making radical changes to my life could be derailed, subconsciously or at times even consciously. There was never any wavering in my love or in my conviction that I wanted our lives, hearts, and souls to be inextricably entwined for as long as possible.

Your move to San Francisco, coupled with

Sacrifice

the uncertainty of how long you might stay there, confused me, introducing all sorts of doubts. This coincided with the fallout caused by my job-seeking activities in the Australian wine industry, as well as a period during which the children were experiencing some difficulties in coming to terms with their new life in a new home, without a resident dad! I felt like a novice highwire artist on his first major walk across the Grand Canyon. I started out confident, staring straight ahead, with an eye on the goal, and with the elation that comes from taking risks, and the knowledge of much pleasure and achievement ahead. But a gust of wind, a small falter in the step, and suddenly I start to look down, and lose faith in my ability to continue. I worry about what's on the other side. Scared by the prospect of falling, I invariably turn back to the shelter from where I started.

It's just turned midnight, and I am now 45 years old. Three bloody cheers!

Anyway where was I? Oh yes, San Francisco. I now realize just what an important phase it has been in your life. An adventure of discovery in many ways, as you say. And I can understand what you meant when you said that if I had come for that long weekend, it would have intruded on that special adventure and all that it meant. However, that period of change of venue, of time zones, and of feelings, culminating in the cancellation of my trip, seemed to have a profound effect. I genuinely thought that it was your way of saying that the emotional strain of it all was proving too much, and that you had to break free and give yourself (ourselves) another chance to look again at our lives and how we ought to lead them. The fact that you had found a friend to sweep away the boredom of isolation, and to introduce you to fun evenings and intimate moments, only fueled my frustration and fear that I wouldn't make that journey to greener pastures, new lives, and unconditional love. I was upset that you thought that I had misled you all this time, or that you were my ticket to Australia. Neither implication is true nor fair.

My desire to live in Australia is enhanced beyond measure by the thought that my life could ultimately be with you, enjoying the level of contentment, and happiness that we have dreamt about, and written about over the past last year. Since that magical romantic and truly wonderful week in Bordeaux, and in London when our two hearts met and merged. But to move to Australia, with all that it involves from the point of view of family, employment, and finances, cannot be undertaken lightly. The development of our relationship was and is inextricably linked. The timing has to be right, and my higher self needs to be telling me when that is.

18th July
Well, I never did get to finish this yesterday, though the day was enhanced beautifully by my talking to you on the telephone twice! And the

arrival of twelve magnificent red roses and a box of chocolates, timeless symbols of love, just had me smiling, grinning, in an office flooded by sunshine. Thank you so very much. Their beauty, aroma and appeal are only exceeded by your beauty, aroma and appeal! And even the thorns seem vaguely familiar! I had a good birthday in many ways, even though I was working. I was in a happy mood and all seemed well. People were kind and I got lots of phone calls, cards and a few presents. I was tired by the time I returned to the flat.

Here we are already two days from starting the letter—sorry! Anyway, back to the events surrounding your time in San Francisco. I felt so confused because I seemed to be receiving such contradictory messages, and I thought I had lost you. We both needed to sort things out and allow our lives to come to terms with enforced and prolonged separation and lingering doubts about the future. I thought that what we had experienced was a glorious, but finite time in our lives during which we discovered ourselves a bit more, and opened up parts of our souls and emotions that had been dormant. Deep down, I don't think I have lost the faith. What we share, the love we have sparked and have nurtured all this time, is just too special and rare. It will transcend obstacles and even time, I'm sure.

I've known Sarah through wine trade circles for quite some time. A few weeks ago we got to talking about our various personal circumstances.

She recently separated from her husband after four years of marriage and a further six years of living with him. They had no children. She broke free from a stifling, boring, complacent life devoid of spark, even though he loved her deeply. I was able to sympathize and offer her the opportunity to talk it through. She was also a sympathetic and friendly listener to my emotional difficulties. I confided in her my love for you and how I thought it was all slipping away. We got on very well and met for the odd movie or dinner after a wine trade function (she is a wine trade journalist). When she told me she had booked a vacation for a week to a villa in Portugal by herself, and asked me if I would care to come, it seemed like a lovely idea. We had fun, and yes we did end up sleeping together, albeit in a single bed! We relaxed, and laughed a lot. We ate a lot of local fish and drank local wine, and enjoyed some much needed physical attention before we returned to the harsh reality of daily life.

I know Sarah has feelings for me, perhaps more than she wants to. She knows and feels that I constantly think of you. Despite the fun we have, and the ease with which we get along, I know that the truly special and unique feelings I have for you cannot be replicated. I would be a liar if I didn't admit that it is nice to have a close friend that I can see from time to time, or phone to share a joke, or go see a movie with, or have sex with. It's something I've craved for so long.

I don't know where it's going to lead. I don't

Sacrifice

love her. I cannot feel the feelings I experience when I'm with you, when I think of you and what we share. She is frightened by her own feelings because she senses they are not truly reciprocated. It is fun to have her as a friend and companion, even though she lives as far south of London as I am north, approximately 130 kilometers away. I would like to continue the friendship, provided we can somehow understand our feelings for each other.

I regret not telling you about my week away before I left. I was not intending to keep the truth from you, especially as I have always appreciated and respected the honesty you have shown me over the months, about everything. I guess my feelings were so very jumbled up, and it coincided with your departure from San Francisco. Anyway, I'm sorry if all this has upset you. It was not my intention. I've rambled as usual and I fear I may not have adequately described how my feelings have been stuck on an emotional roller coaster ride.

I have been back to the aromatherapist. She is helping me to find my higher self, which will take me where I want to go. It has been so good to be back in contact with you, now that you're on home territory. The calls and faxes are very therapeutic, and they brighten my life and enrich me. I do miss you and I miss the bond we have and the way we make love.

I hope it will not be too long before I can see you again, as I want to kiss you so badly.

No doubt this letter will cross with yours, so it will be interesting to read how you're feeling. We'll compare notes soon.

Take care, be happy,
much love to you,
Michael

As the weeks passed after my arrival back to Australia, the emotional desert I seemed to have found myself in stretched far in every direction. I felt lost, disoriented, unfulfilled, and barren. I could only ascertain that what I was going through was still a part of the journey, the last leg after San Francisco.

Coming down from the mountain over the other side was hard, and the loneliness I felt was compounded both professionally and emotionally. It was evident that a lot of my clients had lost faith in me with my numerous jaunts overseas in the past year. I didn't blame them. I just wasn't there when they needed me. Though many remained faithful, some thought that I was gone for good this time, so they referred prospective clients in other directions. And I could not ignore the fact that I came back to the same old routine of doing it all by myself. I could not continue working on my own forever. I craved interaction with other people and my creative isolation was crushing my spirit.

All the feelings I'd put aside over the past two months came flooding back in an intensity of longing. I reflected on the men I'd met over the past three years, and none came even close to what I felt for Michael. I felt as though a lot of emotional ghosts had been laid to rest in San Francisco, and now I was ready for another committed relationship. Moreover I wanted it. Our

Sacrifice

relationship would always be there, simmering, waiting to be turned up to full heat, as we had done in the past.

I could not move on. Every waking moment I seemed to be locked into the possibility of a new life with him. I could not rid this thought from my head and consequently could not concentrate on getting on with business, or other matters. It made sense to me that I should address my emotional needs, and then surely everything else would simply fall into place.

His letters still held me bound to him, and his words made love to me the way no other man had or could. It was clear that we either had to end it or get on with it. I wrote to Michael and asked him for an ultimatum.

July 24th 1996
Michael,

I don't know what to do. I'm lonely without your contact and feelings of love. I'm frustrated at not being close to you physically. I'm scared of commitment, and the binds it brings. And I'm disillusioned about our future. We both have to want to be together for it to occur, with both of us facing our deepest fears. They say you attract to you what you fear the most so that it can be addressed, but it seems that sorting through it all is so very difficult when we are so far apart.

Like a game of chess, I am awaiting your next move, Michael. I feel cornered, not by you, but my own emotions.

Damn you, Michael, for not seizing the day! And I double-damn myself for giving up the front row seats. Either set me free, Michael, or please make the dreams a reality.

*I still love you,
Barbara*

30th July 1996
My dear Barbara,

The letter I started on Sunday has been consigned to the waste bin! The last few days have not been good. I have been feeling very depressed and lack focus. Last night and today were just as bad. I had a session planned with my aromatherapist and somehow she was able to calm me and help me

Sacrifice

get matters back in perspective. I returned home, cooked some lamb cutlets, potatoes and cabbage, ran a hot bath with drops of therapeutic oils, and now here I am, back at the table, putting pen to paper, thinking of you, awakening to a new day. Sometimes the best laid plans do not turn out quite as one would have hoped. The last few months have been hard for us both, haven't they? So much seems to have conspired to frustrate my plans and undermine my confidence. And you find yourself not knowing how to move your life forward.

I have tried to analyze my innermost thoughts time and time again. I always seem to come to the same conclusion. I haven't fulfilled the dream and jumped on a plane and come to live in Australia. Not because of any commitment to my employers, not because of concerns for my wife, not because of hurting the family, not because of any lessening of the strong and wonderful love I have for you, not because I want to develop a relationship with someone else, and not because I feared I might not get a decent job in Australia, but because of a feeling that I could not yet leave the children. The more I think about it, the more straightforward it is. After all, I can break my contract anytime. My wife can fend for herself, and the family will get over it. I still love you and nothing compares. I'm sure I could get a job as a supermarket clerk. However, the time is not yet right to leave the children as I had hoped it would be.

With a heavy heart my dear Barbara, I am

suggesting that we let go, and draw to a close a chapter in this romantic intense mysterious, yet compelling adventure. We are not saying "goodbye," but "au revoir." I have not lost the faith. Perhaps destiny does have us together one day, just not yet. Perhaps, the adventure can take place all over again, without the geographical frustrations. But to be honest, I need to find the right time to start Chapter Two, and in the meantime I cannot expect you to wait in emotional limbo. I need to direct my energies and focus on listening to my higher self, to ensure that I am happy with the direction I am taking. Everything else will fall into place.

Your fax yesterday talked of your life, and work, and having to move on—big steps that you need to take. I entirely understand this and, as always, I admire your courage and your ability to relish the challenge of new opportunities, new places, new friends and new experiences. I really do admire those qualities in you, and I am learning slowly to find those qualities in myself. Sometimes the plans don't go quite right. San Francisco perhaps. So you pick yourself up, dust yourself off, take the good parts with you and start afresh. I'm sure that whatever you do will work out. You deserve to succeed, and my love for you will continue. I wish only the best for you. Something deep inside me sees us together one day. Our lives and our feelings for each other are richer and more meaningful because of the highs and the lows we have endured

Sacrifice

individually and together over these months.

If fate decrees otherwise, whatever happens, my life, my soul, my every strand of body and consciousness has benefited from the love we have shared, and the adventure and road we have travelled. My love for you, and my respect for you as an individual, will never diminish. It is strong and the roots run deep. Like an old vine, it can survive flood, drought, pests, and too much or too little sun. This vine is hardy, and even if it remains dormant for a while, it can still flourish again given the right conditions, developing abundant fruit time and again.

I propose to recommence my search for work in Australia at some time in the future. I guess I will know when the time is right, and when circumstances are favorable. And even then, I do not expect to be able to just walk into your life. It would be nice to think of a romance starting all over again, if that were possible, and if we were able to rekindle the embers of a love that will always burn.

I do not expect you to wait with bated breath, putting your social, emotional, sexual, professional, and family life on hold. I'm only sorry that I have disappointed you thus far. I have never wanted to mislead or deceive you. I hope that one day we can be together, to fulfill each other. But if for any reason, it is not to be, then I will see you in the next life.

I hope we can still correspond often, and keep

each other company on the paths we tread. I'll call you soon, dear Barbara.

*All my love,
Michael*

It was not the answer I wanted to read. I clung to him, desperate to experience the relationship we only wrote about and savored from time to time. I wanted to let the love in fully.

I cried out, "Oh, Michael, is this really what you want?"

He said, "Of course it isn't, but I can't see any other way around it."

"I'm not ready to let go, Michael. I really want this relationship to work!"

But neither of us really knew what to do, or where to take it. We could only keep writing. It was all we had. And so the letters began again. The letters filled only a portion of the huge void in my life. I knew it was not enough. My soul was literally crying out for love, and I began to feel a certain desperation over a seemingly hopeless situation. But I also accepted that he had moved on and understood his feelings of commitment to his children's well being. I resolved that I had better get on with my life.

It is said that there is no greater aphrodisiac than loneliness. Life went on as it does. In the supermarket one day, over the apples, I encountered a nice young man. I felt a positive physical connection from somewhere deep in the pit of my stomach. As we eyed each other in the aisles, each going in opposing directions but meeting halfway back down in the next, I began to feel a hunger, and it wasn't for food. I wanted to get to know this man cruising the aisles in the supermarket. He checked out

Sacrifice

at the register next to me, and we were smiling broadly at each other by this time. I've always found it amusing that when one is attracted to someone, a knowing smile creeps onto their face. Or had someone pinned that nasty joke on my back again (I'm up for it any time buddy!) as I walked through the market, because he was patiently waiting for me outside the market.

"Coffee?" he asked, smiling suggestively at me, knowing we both wanted more.

"Yeah, why not?" I replied.

I should have said no, and walked away with him salivating, my pride intact. We had coffee, not sex, but unlike the boy I'd been dating before I went to Bordeaux and met Michael, this one had a mind and we could converse.

So began my friendship with Anthony, who was fifteen years my junior. He had quite a spiritual bent to him and I found his innocent wisdom to be a small light in my life. The friendship gave me the human contact I needed, but it was not enough. He made me realize that I needed someone to laugh with, to read to, to cook for, to cycle with, to dance with, to sing badly to, and explore new places and have brave new experiences with.

When we did go dancing, he'd end up going home with someone his own age, which I was fine with. I can't say I blamed him. How the hell was I ever going to compete with a girl in her twenties anyway? It did not do wonders for my ego, but I also just wasn't into him. If *the woman* does not have the right receptors out, then it's never going to happen. *The woman* often seems to be the predetermining factor in whether a relationship works or not. This one quite clearly was not going anywhere. Though he was nice-looking, the age difference conspired against us and it made me crave Michael even more. I send him a card, just to say *'hi'*...thats all!

12th August 1996
Dear Barbara,

Your card arrived today. The photo of Sydney Harbour on Australia Day 1988 brought back so many memories of when I celebrated the bicentenary of Australia in 1988 with my wife. Very mixed ones actually. I was on the harbor that very evening, watching the crowds, the boats, and the splendid fireworks. We were all wearing dinner jackets. Some of our friends from the North Shore were with us. We were dressed a bit too formally for the occasion. Secretly I wanted to be on the shoreline, on the rocks perhaps, or on Macquarie Point, with the Sydneysiders and a beer. Not a glass of champagne and a canapé!

Anyway, my wife was below deck chatting to friends. I was on the deck alone, staring at the wondrous sight of Sydney, vowing that I would be back one day. It was January, 1988 and although I didn't know then the exact date of our return to the UK, I knew it would be that year. We were only supposed to be there for three years. I really didn't want to go back. I knew my wife did, and I feared

Sacrifice

that a further extension of my exile from company headquarters would harm my career, so I didn't fight to stay longer. Another example perhaps in retrospect of my reluctance to follow gut feelings, catering instead to an absurd sense of responsibility and loyalty to every Tom, Dick and Harry. Loyalty and honor are admirable traits of course, but when faced with a beautiful opportunity, one should grasp it. And Sydney's not so bad either!

Hearing you on the phone this morning, telling me how good Sydney felt, was a lovely way to brighten a dour Monday. I envy you, but I'll be back too one day! I'm listening to the Gloria Estefan CD you sent me, 'Destiny'. I love the songs, especially the lyrics. There's much more I want to write. I will put it all in a letter soon.

Lovely to hear your voice today. I wanted to give you a big hug and an even bigger kiss.

Much love,
Michael

Anthony wandered in and out of my life on an irregular basis. It was never going to become anything other than a friendship. It was insufficient and lacked real intimacy. Instead of helping me get over Michael, it only seemed to enhance my need for a really committed relationship.

I had just installed a modem on my computer and wanted to use my new toy, so I found myself writing quick newsy emails off to Michael every day. I did not know where we stood anymore emotionally. He had someone else now. But he was always quick to respond and seemed to relish the regular contact again. His words of love seemed to indicate that he still cared deeply for me. I was absorbed by the need for his contact. Was he reaching out for me again? I wanted and needed to belong again, but I was so terribly confused.

During the course of the relationship, we regularly sent each other what we affectionately called *'fuck tapes'*. They were compilations of our favorite songs, both raunchy and touching. There were love songs, and sometimes opera. It was a form of expressing our feelings for each other through music, since geography was such an obstacle. I enjoyed making them as much as I did receiving them. I hadn't made one since before I left for San Francisco and thought it would be an appropriate way of showing Michael how much I loved him. Deep down I felt I wanted the relationship to work somehow. I knew we could overcome the geography factor, but one of us needed to make some personal sacrifices. Ironically, he had also made a tape, and they crossed in the mail. We must have made them at exactly the same time. I felt he was reaching out to me also. The songs were soulful and mellow, and the words were an elixer for my aching heart.

He had gone to Majorca with his children during their summer holiday, and had not yet received mine. Over the course of the following week while he was in Spain, I thought long and hard about the possibility of moving to London so that we could start a life together. I discussed it with my children. Having already been through the prospect of my impending departure to the States, they thought it was radical. At sixteen and eighteen, all they could really think about was holidays abroad. They were a lot further down the track emotionally with our separation

Sacrifice

than Michael's children. In a way it made sense that I should be the one to make the move, in light of our respective children's dispositions. London had some great design studios, which I was confident I could find work in, further enhancing my professional career and solving my creative isolation as well.

I shared my thoughts on moving to London with Michael and he thought it made perfect sense too. The puzzle was finally falling into place. So it seemed.

27th August 1996
Dear Barbara,

Well, we're sitting here at Palma Airport on Majorca. There is only one hour to go before the flight leaves and surprise, surprise, there is no 'delayed' sign up on the board, yet! I'll only believe it when we are actually up in the air.

The rest of the week passed by with much the same routine. Sleep until nine, breakfast, pool, beach, pool, sun, lunch, sun, pool, drinks on the balcony, playing cards with the children, dinner, entertainment outside, bed about midnight, and me usually with a headache from too much crappy local wine. Both children made some friends their own age and were sad to leave them, everyone promising to write frequently, which I doubt, but you never know. I can safely say that I met no one that I will keep in touch with.

Back in England 11:30pm.

Well, the flight was not delayed, thank goodness. Back to cool and overcast England. Calling via the office to collect your package. I'm listening to the tape now, and have devoured your letter twice already. The tape is great, as I knew it would be.

So many shared feelings, as always. I loved your letter. You express yourself so well, and I am still deeply in love with you. The times during the holiday that I was able to sit and think about us only confirmed just how much I care for you. I know you know that. We both know only too well what spoiled our respective marriages. We know our faults, those of our partners, though some only in retrospect. We know the dangers, the pitfalls, and we recognize what is needed in a relationship, and what has to be avoided. Complacency in all its forms. We also know that the 'higher plane' is worth striving for. I want to offer you the chance to be womanly, yet be free enough to develop your unique individual strength of character, and also explore a path that allows us to mature together, blending in a positive way. Above all, loving, laughing, living, learning, caressing, confiding, giving, growing, helping, healing, understanding,

Sacrifice

undressing, being patient, generous, strong, individual, creative, kind, generous, daring, different and in love, on a higher plane.

We want it so much, don't we?

I love you Barbara,
Michael

8th September 1996
Dear Michael,

I do hope that this is what you want too, and that I am not thwarting your plans to immigrate to Oz. It was a decision which seemed to culminate after my job-searching in Sydney, during which time, as you know, I found myself continually thinking of you, of us.

I feel so sure that I want to be with you. A relationship and true companionship seems more important to me than new solo adventures right now. I am sure that the exact location of our new home will evolve, and England will reveal lots of surprises for us both. Australia in our hearts, the ultimate goal being Sydney in 2000, which is where I know you also want to be, celebrating with the other Aussies under the bridge, beer in one hand, me in the other, fireworks exploding over the magnificent harbor and in our hearts. We could hoist a couple of posts 10 feet from the water's edge at Kirribilli House and make a tent between them. I'm sure the PM won't mind!

I know the dream is not far away now, Michael. Besides, you shall have your very own piece of Australia to take to bed with you every night, and I am so desperate for our lovemaking. How I have missed it.

There is so much more to be revealed, I know. I have been reading all your letters and faxes recently. They touch my heart. While reading one letter, which mentioned you were listening to 'Hope Has a Place' by Enya, guess what started playing (random selection) and is playing now (random again)! The music and words to the songs we have shared, do help connect us, of that I am sure. We must have been making the tapes at exactly the same time last week. In sync and in harmony. Just like the music.

Again, I can't help but feel scared and excited all at once. I know we have a special combination, one that not many find and I know it has the right ingredients to last forever. If either one of us falters along the way, please let honesty, integrity and respect be the key to sustaining our love and helping each other when we need it. I do want to retain that specialness. The sort you witness when

Sacrifice

you see two old people walking down the street hand in hand. Or a couple groping on the ground in a park. The way you looked at me and touched my heart (or was it my breasts) at Ransom's Dock? The way you kissed me at the window, that first night of our meeting in Bordeaux, sat me on your knee at Oakleigh Court, and made passionate love to me at the hotel on the Rhône. I feel wonderful with the anticipation of sharing such a love with someone I love to the depths of my soul. It is rare, Michael.

This has been an eventful year hasn't it? I need to know that this is what you want, too. I don't wish to be guilty of orchestrating your life. Please think carefully about all I am offering before I set the ball in motion, because once I do, I pull out all stops.

With Love,
Barbara

16th September 1996
Dear Barbara,

I am sitting here listening to Boz Scaggs, thinking of you waking, rising, showering and preparing for your day. I'm thinking how much better Monday mornings will be when we're together! I was lying on the sofa looking up at the ceiling, imagining what it will be like when we are together. When destiny finally puts the jigsaw pieces into place. I am so longing to start that chapter.

Barbara, my body and soul aches for your company, your love. We need each other and I reckon we deserve each other too! It seems odd that the original plan for me to move continents has turned around. It is now you who are making that journey. But I feel that this will be the right prelude for our future together. The fact that you are making that commitment means so much to me, and I will always remember that. I still yearn to live in Australia with you one day, and I know we will. I can see it. I have always seen it. We will be so happy there.

Sacrifice

In the meantime, we start out in the hustle and bustle of England. There will be some challenges but there will be many adventures too. All will be well, because we want it to happen. We can restore the passion in our hearts and souls as we leap.

I am acutely aware of your disappointment that I did not seize the day and make the journey to Adelaide. I often lie awake at nights, thinking of the circumstances surrounding the last few months, including the San Francisco episode. Your suggestion of coming to England for a short spell is a sacrifice that touches me deeply. I know you realized how big a leap it would be for me to leave family and business if I came to Australia. So I understand how you must feel about making a similar jump! The prospect of our being able to start a wonderful journey sooner by your coming here for a short while, and helping your career in the process, is immensely exciting and fills my heart with glee. The prospect of Sydney in 2000, or much sooner I hope, is such a powerful thought. I have often dreamed of us at The Rocks, smiling at each other, toasting our adventure. I am confident that somehow we will work it out so that we are happy, and our respective children and careers will benefit from our route to happiness born out of our love.

We'll find the way, and how sweet it will be when we get there.

Michael

September 22nd 1996
Dear Michael,

I am so glad that we are on the same wave length again. On the Christmas front, happy to not be there to complicate family issues with all the external pressure that can bring. It is important to me that we start off on a good footing, with as little as possible conflict from outside factors. We are both aware of the emotional forces which can interfere at a deeper level than we care to admit, from family. Although I would love to have a white Christmas with you, I shall have to make do with lovely thoughts of the future.

I am adamant about being there to see the New Year in. For once in my life the event will actually signify something new! I shall try to book a flight on either Boxing Day, or the 29th of December. From midsummer to midwinter, into your arms, your bed, and your life. Our lives. I want this so much, Michael. You expressed some anxiety when we last spoke. I hope you are not having second thoughts. Are you?

It has been a very uneventful weekend. Early

Sacrifice

nights, plenty of sleeping in. I managed to psych myself into a couple of aerobics classes, some retail therapy, furniture painting, general goofing around, and a lot of daydreaming. I'm not lonely, because I love you and I know that you love me. Instead I am enjoying my aloneness, knowing that it will end soon, relishing it for what it is, and appreciating it for the contrast it will bring in time. Sharing the intimacy. Being in your space, and you in mine. More importantly, the aloneness makes me want you all the more. I am enjoying my little townhouse. The rustle of the wind in the gum trees at the back, Felix, my sole companion and friend, stretched out on the back doorstep. Reflecting, on solitude, times gone by and what the future may bring.

This is another reason why I wanted to wait until December. My own test. I have always done things impromptu, like when I came to Australia, I'd made up my mind and was packed and gone in two weeks. Perhaps the same could be said of the San Francisco venture. I 'just do it' (albeit without much foresight!)

This time I want to be absolutely sure, I want to do this properly, methodically, and with regard for both of our respective families' feelings rather than our own, having come this far.

I found some great quotes by Breck Costin that I liked. Some 'food for thought', though I am sure that saying should really mean 'thought for food'!

"Put at risk what you have become, for the possibility of all that you could be, whether the goal is building extraordinary relationships or creating important partnerships."

"Restore passion in the heart & soul."

"Look if you like, but you will have to leap."... Breck Costin.

Bring it on...
Barbara

17th October 1996
My dear Barbara,

I was glad that I had a session with the aromatherapist this evening. She was able to help reinforce some of the self-belief and trusting disciplines that seem to have forsaken me of late. The massage oils, which I'm sure she had strengthened this time, caused me to have a weird variety of visions. Initially they were bizarre. Quite disturbing and hostile faces, like gargoyles, surrounded by sinister blue. But they faded and gave way to other people,

Sacrifice

none of whom I recognized. They got progressively friendlier and more benign and the colors changed to more positive yellows, rose and light blues. My faith, positivity and mellow calm led me out of the dark and stormy night.

I left there with a sense of calm and with renewed faith in my ability to communicate with my higher self. To discard negative thoughts as one would swat an annoying fly. I came back to the flat with a smile and pottered about. I cooked a meal, poured a glass of wine and set about reading from the huge file of our letters, faxes and cards. It was exactly a year ago that I prepared for my visit last November. I am as excited now as I was then, though much has happened since.

What amused me (a trivial point) was that I noticed that the file in which I keep all the correspondence is the one I used in the office when I first exchanged faxes with you about your Vinexpo trip. They were quite formal, weren't they? Anyway to identify the file, I had just written 'Harkness' on the cover. It was an old file that my secretary had used once. I had put some correspondence in it after a holiday and she had written 'requiring action' on it! It made me smile as I looked at it, and I said, "Yes, you bet!"

Dear Barbara, I'm sorry that you have felt the negative energy over the past few days. I was glad for the opportunity to talk about it on the phone, although I fear that in my sleepy state, my muddled thoughts may not have made as much sense as I *would have liked. Yesterday I was in a bad way, for a variety of reasons. But I have been able to view things from a much more positive perspective today. I look forward to our being able to hold each other. To reaffirm all those beautiful things, both physical and emotional, that have bound us together these last sixteen months, through many highs and lows. I spent so much time reading the letters and some of the extracts from books and sayings that you sent over the months, that I hardly noticed how late it was getting. I hope this letter helps to make your Friday a good day. The most important thing is that my love for you is as strong as ever. I want to feel you close so that all the positive energy can charge us until we glow in the dark! Take care. This comes with a huge hug and a passionate kiss.*

All my love and more,
Michael

Sacrifice

October 26th 1996
Dear Michael,

It has been a while since I wrote you a long soulful letter, and it is long overdue. It is easy with modern communication methods to get a quick fix, but handwritten letters, messy as they sometimes are, feel like they come from the heart somehow.

My visa came through on Friday. It is lovely, and would make a nice wine label. I seem to see wine labels in everything! It is dated October 1st, so I shall remember to celebrate gaining my UK residency when it is my son's birthday as well. I am getting excited about living in England itself, apart from living with you, which falls into a totally different category. All the possibilities of being on the other side of the world, the olde worlde—with all its majesty, magnificence and decay are quite alluring. The antithesis of Australia.

I am re-reading a lot of my old books. A kind of affirmation to the personal growth I have undergone in the past three years since I left the marriage. They have all helped me in small ways to understand the mysteries of life. I am so fortunate at the moment to have this free space around me. I think it is overdue, and began when I went to San Francisco. Now I am in this state of blissfulness. Content in the knowledge of our future, confident about who I am, especially when I am with you, and thankful that we have found in each other, a love so profound and deep. I am slightly curious about my professional future, but not pursuing that too fervently. I have learned recently that you can't push things, and that going with the flow is a much better way of letting things work themselves out.

I found a quote in the book Soulmates by Thomas Moore that I found pertinent to my parents' marriage, my own marriage, and possibly yours, too.

"Oddly, the attempts of many married people to create an affluent environment, might even be the cause of marital failure, because the point in marriage is not to create a material world, but rather to evoke a spirit of love that is not of this world."

This inner calm is having quite a profound effect on my sleeping habits. For the first time in literally years, I am having solid nights of sleep. I am quite amazed! I'm not sure whether it's my own personal surrender, or the stressless lifestyle I am now leading. Anyway, it's fabulous and I'm catching up on years of sleep deprivation.

About being confidant of who I am: a huge part of who I am is my sexuality. I now know that this was why I needed to leave my marriage. I was not able to express myself within it. I'm never happier than when I have occasion to glam up, even if there is nowhere to go, preferably in something sexy. I know that men admire me, and I like the act of flirting, I find it quite empowering. I know that you understand and appreciate this part of my nature and that you enjoy it as well. But mostly, I feel happy about being able to share my sexuality with someone I trust so implicitly. There is so much about me and about you, that is the unique combination of two souls, adoring and loving the qualities that make... us.

I love you Michael and I love being loved by you.

Barbara

Barely a day went by that we were not in contact. Especially now that we could correspond via email. So when nothing came through for five whole days, I knew something was wrong. I don't know whether it was the blaring obviousness or not, but I seemed to sense a "shift" somehow. When I rang Michael to ask what was wrong, he could not deny the truth, and told me he had been seeing a therapist, for a multitude of reasons.

"You do still love me, don't you?" I asked.

"Yes. Yes, of course I do. Nothing has changed my feelings for you," he replied, which did reassure me. "I think I've had a sort of minor nervous breakdown!"

I wasn't expecting this. My heart felt heavy with the realization that I didn't know him well enough. I thought I did. I thought the letters revealed his true self, but in fact they also created a pseudo-relationship based on what we wanted to believe. Had Michael been deluding me all this time? Was the reality of our relationship and the impending commitment all too much to bear? Had he only been telling me what he thought I wanted to hear in his letters?

He reassured me that everything would be all right. But he also intimated that he wanted to come out to Australia for a holiday and see me, just to be sure before I packed up for a life in England with him. I believed him.

This was surely just a minor, last-minute hiccup?

***

I was at the airport early. The London flight via Singapore usually got into Adelaide around 6:30 a.m. I did not want to be late like last time, so I was glad to be waiting along with the other early arrivals.

I like watching people. Australian people in particular have such an honesty about them. I found myself thinking how much I would miss this country. But that thought paled into insignificance when it came to the desire to be with Michael, and the whole new adventure we were about to embark upon, wherever it was taking us. Australia would always be here, and we knew we'd live here again together one day. I was excited by this prospect. As if any minute now he would walk through those gates, and the cameras would start rolling again, and I would become the leading lady, with my leading man, our adventure playing out once more upon the stage.

There he was, and here he is, holding me, kissing me, reality

Sacrifice

at last. Bliss. The first hours together after a five-month long separation were delicious. I suggested he have a shower to freshen up after the long journey, and promptly joined him. It was nice just touching and soaping each other's bodies, getting to know all the familiar details again. Feelings and emotions that hours ago were only memories.

There is such ecstasy in abstinence. Knowing there will be fulfillment when the lovemaking finally occurs releases such pent-up torrents of passion.

One of the aspects of a relationship I find intriguing is the marriage of food and love. When in love, I want to experiment with all sorts of delicacies and recipes I have never tried. I go about planning menus and dinners for friends and use them like culinary guinea pigs. They never seem to mind. For lunch the day Michael arrived, I made a smoked salmon salad with lightly steamed asparagus, over a mixture of lettuce, sprinkled with pan-fried, crisp capers. We sat down in my small courtyard in the hot Australian November sun under the big market umbrella, accompanied of course by delicious South Australian wine.

Michael didn't eat. He just sat there without touching his food. Although I knew he was experiencing a degree of emotional trauma, I was still not prepared for this change in the script.

"What's wrong?," I asked.

Silence.

"I don't want you to come to England to live with me," came the stoic reply.

Quite suddenly, my stomach did a double back flip, my fork fell to the ground and the whole world went into slow motion as I tried to comprehend what he was telling me.

"I think I have lost the conviction...I'm unsure that it would work if you came to London...I feel that it is too soon after my marriage for another committed relationship...I think that I should experience other women...I'm sorry"

It came out in a stupefying single phrase of broken sentences, or should I say excuses?

Then he added, "I feel that I need to live a life of solitude for a while, without your letters and phone calls."

His words and behavior smacked of psychotherapy.

"You came all the way out to Australia to tell me this? Surely you could have said this in a letter, and saved yourself the airfare!" I was absolutely perplexed by this fact.

"I wanted to see you again, to see if the spark could ignite. I had to be sure," he said.

His telling me so early in the week, meant that he had thought about it considerably. He was not willing to spend any more time to try to reignite the fire. Suddenly, all his letters felt like volumes of deceit.

I didn't know how or what to feel. After the world stopped spinning, and the numbness subsided, there were feelings of having been cheated, topped with anger, then mingled with sadness and regret. Overcome with emotion, I finally decided that I felt completely devastated.

I felt like crawling into a ball and rolling quietly away, unnoticed.

The lunch was tossed in the bin, uneaten. I stormed upstairs to collect my clothes for our weekend in the Clare Valley.

I had organized all sorts of romantic journeys to different locations, just like his last visit. We set off to Thorn Park in the Clare Valley, an ideal setting, renowned for its romantic hideaway guest houses. The special magic had gone from Michael's persona. The electrical charge no longer coursed between us.

Michael was totally preoccupied with family problems in

Sacrifice

England, wallowing in his guilt over ruining his wife's and children's lives. He felt overburdened by his responsibility for the well-being of people who relied on him. This was all he talked about during the one-hour trip north to the Clare Valley, a wine disrict 100kms north of Adelaide. I could see now, that my going to London would have created an added responsibility for him. Perhaps this is what set off his alarm bells. But my decision was based on love and a desire to take the relationship to the next stage if we were to progress at all, and I thought this was what Michael wanted too. I so wanted to experience the Michael I thought I knew. We were still able to make love, though not feeling as gentle and romantic as we'd felt in the past. I secretly hoped that a spark would ignite and all those feelings would fire him up again. That he would find conviction through our lovemaking. I held onto my faith that we would sort it out somehow. But by the third day, I needed my fears allayed. My questions led to the answers I did not want to hear.

"Why did you start writing to me again after I returned from San Francisco?"

"All I wanted was a sign from you, Barbara, and you gave it to me. I was still in love with you. I still wanted you."

"But you made it all seem as though you wanted it so desperately, too?" I replied.

"I thought I did. I don't know. I just feel that England would have destroyed us."

"So I came with a covenant, and Australia was part of it, wasn't it?"

"Yes...no, it's you. I felt that I could not give you what you really deserve in a relationship, that you would eventually leave me and blame me for destroying your life in Australia, and all that you have built here."

"Well, that's very noble of you Michael, but I thought we were doing this for each other!" I said hastily.

Michael stated feelings of emotional inadequacy, which I found hard to believe in light of his letters. I did not understand his confession, for the fact that he was doing so much work on himself, possibly too much, was one of the things I admired about him and openly encouraged. I was not aware that I induced these feelings in him—quite the opposite, in fact.

I felt some deep karmic connection between Michael, myself, and our respective partners. He'd told me that he now understood how his wife must have felt in their marriage as she'd had feelings of inadequacy in their relationship. And now I was experiencing the same feelings my husband must have felt when I left, by Michael ending it before we'd even begun. The repercussions of cause and effect were such that each of us began to feel something our previous partners must have experienced as a result of our own past actions.

I was acutely aware that Michael and I had reached our crescendo and that our meeting in this lifetime was to be lived only on a higher plane, with brief visits to either sides of the earth for some mortal pleasures. It was a relationship which took place not only in the stratosphere, through telephones, telepathy, faxes and good old-fashioned letters, but also in our minds, hearts, and our souls, which could not be matched by the mundane state of a daily existence. I knew he still loved me, but by not continuing the relationship we saved the love and respect that we had for each other. He was afraid that his own human shortcomings would dissolve my vision of the man he had become in his letters. He was afraid we could not live out the dream as realized and would therefore rather it remain just that, a dream, which lives on forever.

Sacrifice

I did believe that what he felt for me was the sort of love marriages are based on, and that we were both swept away at the time with the romance of it all. When he described how he thought he had broken the mould of conjugality, I knew that his true self was finally emerging, and encouraged him not to fight these fears but to listen to them for they were his higher self saying "No."

On the fourth day, Michael had work commitments in Adelaide and would be gone for the day. I was feeling pretty close to the brink, having bottled up my despair over his change of heart. With him gone for the day I could address how I really felt. I fell apart.

My son came over unexpectedly and caught me unaware. I had dissolved into a blithering mess. Words would not come out properly and he did not know what to do as I sat on the floor against the refrigerator and sobbed uncontrollably. I tried to compose myself temporarily for his benefit, and said, "It's okay, I'll be okay. I won't be going to England, though." He seemed to understand, and left me to it.

But the river of tears would not stop, and I knew I had to talk to someone, otherwise the override switch would trip.

I needed counseling RIGHT NOW! In the past, the only time I have sought clairvoyant advice was when the sublunary didn't seem to answer my questions. I desperately needed to talk to someone with intuition and understanding of the forces that pattern our lives. I looked in the yellow pages (of all places) and found an astrologer who could see me immediatley. She specialized in esoteric, psycho-spiritual, astrology readings. Sounded like she covered just about everything. Even though I had never been into astrology (thinking star signs and horoscopes to be too general) what she had to tell me changed my views considerably. I gave my birth date and time over the phone, so that when I arrived at her house she had my chart all worked out, from a computer program I may add!

The first thing she said to me when she opened her door was, "You should be really very angry! Your life is a complicated mess at the moment, and you have everything coming at you from every direction."

I burst into tears again, and she led me through to her studio. Every aspect of my life was crossed in conflict and yes, the chart did look a bloody mess. I didn't know how she could figure it out, for to me it looked like a really bizarre mass of intersecting lines of string. But that's also exactly how I felt, tied up in knots.

I noticed quickly that she had my birthdate incorrect, a day early. She replied that it was all based on Greenwich Mean Time, and sure enough, London was written underneath that date. There was one lonely part of the chart she had circled that had a male/female symbol together, which she explained meant I was ready for and considering a committed relationship. There were things I took on board and others I chose to discard, as I always do. She suggested I still go to London if I felt the relationship was worth pursuing, but I knew I never would. One thing I had learned from my marriage, and the eight years it took me to leave, was to not leave doors open. Close them, and move on.

Suddenly I wished I had done this when I'd returned from San Francisco. I was not one to enforce my needs or desires on someone because of what *I* wanted. Talking this through with someone exterior to our relationship clarified that I would certainly not pursue the relationship in London. Michael needed his own space and time to truly find himself and what he wanted and I had the greatest respect for his choice. It was a great comfort, however, to know that the universe was responsible.

Sacrifice

Now I knew that every thing was in perfect order.

When Michael came home from his work that day, we fell into each others arms, desperate for love and comfort. We made love for hours, played all our favorite games, and he said for the first time since he arrived, "I love you, Barbara."

But our lovemaking could not change how he felt. I knew this. Something in his soul had shifted and it was causing us both great grief. The sadness engulfing us was excruciatingly painful. My body felt as if someone had walked all over me. I hadn't eaten properly all week. I was extremely hungry, yet the thought of food made me feel sick. Nor could I stop the reservoir of tears which seemed to overflow at their own free will.

My acceptance of his decision left absolutely nothing to talk about, which was an acute reminder of how life does not always work out as you planned. I had imagined us talking about our future, all the mundane details, like which furniture items I would ship over to combine with his, where we'd live, the type of place we might live in, what London had to offer in that respect, family issues and how we might deal with them, and above all, what fun we'd have realizing our dream. But all was said and done. Michael was adamant that I should not go to London, nor should we continue to correspond as we had over the past sixteen months. I knew we couldn't go on like that forever.

After the fifth day, the realization had well and truly sunk in, and the relationship had also sunk to new depths. I was feeling angry. I banished him from my bed that night, after he complained of my *'mood swings'!* I was quite proud of the fact that I had not yet raised my voice in anger, but when I shouted to him, "Get out, you have no idea of the damage you caused both to the relationship and my life!"

It felt cathartic, because I was genuinely angry and upset

about all the reversals which would have to take place both emotionally and practically.

We faced each other the next morning, downstairs, and did not know what to do. We couldn't really kiss and make up. It was all over and we had accepted that.

Every hour of every day, was agony for us both, and so we sat down outside in the garden courtyard and tried to logically sort out what to do next. We both needed to be put out of our misery, (so to speak) and so Michael agreed to return to London three days earlier than scheduled. I came inside and switched on the random selection CD player and *Sting* began to play *Let Your Soul Be Your Pilot*. It was one of the tracks I had included on my last tape for Michael. When I returned, he was gone, but a quick search found him down the side alley of my townhouse, crumpled in a heap on the ground crying.

I knew in an instant that he was following his inner voice, and it grieved him terribly to have lost the commitment to our future so abruptly and surely.

I went to him and offered my hand, helped him up, led him inside and pulled him gently down onto the floor, tenderly placing two large cushions under our heads. Words were inadequate. We had said enough, but the tears felt good. We played some old mellow favorites, then Sacrifice, and held each other tightly, loosely, fondly and sobbed.

I remembered back to a year ago when we had danced around the room to soft music, enjoying our reflection in the windows, feeling the love course between us in our embrace.

And now here we lay crumpled and spent on the floor, not dancing anymore, but embraced by that same love in its death throes. The contrast of emotions so extreme, the pain so acute that I could hardly remember what joy was. I asked Michael why

Sacrifice

he had bothered to come out here when it seemed that he had already resolved his feelings in England. To which he replied, "I had to know for sure, because what we had was so very special."

In a way it was befitting that a relationship such as ours, ethereal as it was, should have an ending experienced in the physical realm. For we could experience the pain together in a real sense and be there for each other to comfort and confide in. I could see that it possibly never would have ended had we kept writing, for it was just too tempting to pick up a pen, or the phone, or of late, correspond by email.

***

That day I took Michael to Carrick Hill, a South Australian National Trust Estate and certainly one of the loveliest homes in Adelaide. The beautiful Carrick Hill Estate was the result of the marriage, in 1935, of Edward (Bill) Hayward and Ursula Barr Smith. Being the offspring of two of Adelaide's most prominent and wealthy families, theirs was undoubtedly the most celebrated Adelaide society wedding of that decade. Edward was the son of a wealthy merchant family that for more than one hundred years had owned John Martin's Ltd, once Adelaide's greatest department store. His bride, Ursula Barr Smith, was a daughter of an even wealthier family of pastoralists. Ursula's father gave the couple the land on which Carrick Hill now stands as a wedding present. Much of the houses interior had been purchased during their honeymoon in England, from a demolition sale of a magnificent country home and shipped back to Adelaide. The building was then architecturally designed around a magnificent Jacobean interior staircase.

Unfortunately the marriage had not produced any children,

but fortunately for the people of South Australia, as the grand estate was bequeathed to the National Trust.

I thought Michael would appreciate Carrick Hill's masterpiece, especially its wonderful gardens filled with sculpture, rose gardens, a maze, sprawling lawns, and high hedges, blending the serenity of old English traditions with the ambience of Australia. Being the quintessential Englishman that he was, Michael loved it, and we sat down to absorb the beauty around us. We certainly needed some sort of distraction from ourselves.

We took a walk afterwards up to Brown Hill, just behind the Estate. From the top, a magnificent view of Adelaide can be seen, encompassing the sea to the west, the hills to the east, and the vast flat plains upon which Adelaide is built in-between. Michael was just as at home there, sitting on the tough dry grass amongst the Paterson's Curse weed, as he was in the English garden of Carrick Hill, possibly more.

We talked a lot about Australia, how it was a country you either loved or hated, that there was no in-between. I think now having read all his letters in an effort to understand the outcome, I realized that Australia was a big part of his dream. Although he had loved me deeply and we both thought that being together, no matter how or where, was of prime importance, I now know that it wasn't. Michael had his own dreams which went a lot further back than our meeting in Bordeaux, and my going to England would have changed all that. Yes indeed, *destiny does not take you where you don't want to go*. I did not have a burning desire to live in England, but I know that I could have done so quite easily, for the love we shared.

However, this was not to be and the realization for me that Adelaide, Australia, was my home was somewhat comforting at that moment. Perhaps things would have gone to plan if it

Sacrifice

had been that simple. I had lived in Adelaide for ten years, the longest I had been in any one place in Australia. My life had been somewhat like a gypsy's. Arriving in Australia twenty-one years ago, I had lived in twelve different locations. Therefore I was adept at adjusting to new environments, which is why I know I could have made the move to England with relative ease.

***

As we woke on the last morning together, I found I could not reach over to touch him. My human wall or defense mechanism had gone up, and I knew there would never be anything physical between us again.

The strangest thing did happen though, as he turned towards me in bed—I swear I saw my father's face. I felt I was lying next to my father and it alarmed and disturbed me somewhat, mainly because of the clarity of the vision. Perhaps that was why I could not bring myself to make love on the last day. I had confided in Michael the fact that he reminded me of my father, though in appearance only, but it never became a perversity in our lovemaking and the thought never entered my head during sex. However, I had to ask myself honestly whether the power of his love was based somewhat on my need to be nurtured and loved with the intensity that Michael had offered because I had been neglected by my father during childhood. I believe all these aspects come into play in relationships we have as adults, and they are not necessarily unhealthy, quite the opposite in fact, if we can realize and address them for precisely what they are.

Lying in bed on that final morning I thought about many things. I was struck by the realization of unconditional love. I think for the first time in my life, besides the love of a mother for her children, I fully understood and appreciated it. I loved Michael deeply, so much that I respected his decision with understanding and could still deal with my own pain of hurt and rejection. After all, they were my feelings of pain, but they did not change how I felt about him. I had been so ready to meld with someone again, but because I had been through my own feelings of doubt about commitment I could empathize with what he was feeling. I had learned through my own experience that if you truly love someone, then you must respect their decisions, their own mind and their emotions. Who are we to impose our wants and needs upon another human being who cannot fulfill them?

My husband had been in denial of my personal growth and wish to leave the marriage, and as a consequence I felt as though I had no voice at all. It is only when we have total freedom within relationship that we can give unconditionally of ourselves.

It is said that the blueprint for any relationship is set within the first few weeks of meeting. For us this was in a foreign country, on holidays, and both of us were searching for love. But to live out a life of reality may have indeed spoiled the love we felt for each other, which was deep and I believe established in an entirely different realm to the *every day*. Not having him physically made me seek and question my perception of love, rather than validate the love through sex. I found it within me and it is within us all.

After my silent morning contemplation, which seemed like an eternity, I turned and said to him, "I am totally at ease with your decision to end the relationship, Michael, for you must do what feels right in your heart, and not what other people expect of you...including me."

Whenever we had parted in the past, I never cried. I had always

Sacrifice

felt confident that we would be together soon, and besides, we'd been on track towards a common goal. I'd always felt that each parting was actually drawing us closer to being together.

This time was very different. The comparison of feelings I'd experienced just one week ago, when I had been at the same location eagerly waiting for him to burst through the arrival gates and experience him physically again, was beyond my range of emotional comprehension. I had tipped into the depths of sadness and despair, unable to experience joy with him any longer. This was very unlike the time twelve months ago when every minute was precious, and we wanted time to stand absolutely still. Now the minutes seemed like hours, and they could not pass quickly enough.

Not relishing his leaving, I was also anxious for him to go. I cherished our last embrace, feeling his huge masculine body envelope me one last time. Then, as if in slow motion, he stood at the departure gates, and turned to face me one last time. I saw that he was crying.

"I love you," he whispered as he passed through and the gates closed shut behind him.

A revelation suddenly occurred to me, that this was the final act, that neither of us ever would make a sacrifice in the material or personal sense. But a sacrifice indeed was made by us both in order to preserve the love and passion of our souls.

BARBARA HARKNESS

For Michael

*Two souls, two hearts,
destined to meet,
drawn to one another
...magnetic love.
He had inner foresight,
she offered the key.
He had been waiting
...patiently.
Passionately, emotionally
they offered their parts
and played them readily.
The paths are not found,
but sought and made,
creating lessons along the way.
Was it to learn how to love?
Was it to learn how to leave?
Or was it just for the love we made.
Were we to know of the torrent released
by the combining of our hearts—our souls.
Were we to know of the pain of separation,
the fullness and emptiness,
companionship and loneliness
the passion and frustration,
the freedom and constraint,
our divineness, our mortality
the truth and the lies.
I didn't know...
but I do know I have loved,
as I've never loved before,
and been loved back by a man so dear,
in a way he'd only dreamed.*

*Life is what happens to you......
while you're busy making other plans.*

John Lennon

EPILOGUE

I made a pact with my soul to never write another letter to Michael. And I didn't. Directly after his departure I shut myself off from the world, bolted away in my townhouse. I also didn't go to work! Launching back into the real world didn't feel right somehow. At night I would light the home with candles, and listen to beautiful classical piano music. This invoked a meltdown of sorts, as I wrapped myself up in a blanket and just sobbed night after night. The tears felt like a necessary cleansing for my soul. In time I stopped doing this, for the crying simply dried up. The self-imposed *'meltdown'* was my intuition instructing me to give in to the flow. Which was more like a raging river in this case.

Eventually I had to hang my shingle back out, for I needed funds to live in the mortal world somehow. A curious thing happened, which I believe could have been just one aspect of what my soul really had in store for me. I put all of my energy (and love) into my business. *'If it is to be, it is up to me'* is what I told myself. The business grew into something much larger than myself, I became really good at what I did and one of my label designs went on to become one of the world's most powerful wine brands.

I believe that the life I ended up leading was the road meant for me. Love was the sacrifice, independence the reward (at that time in my life). I am convinced that leaving my husband, and sabotaging my relationship with Michael was my souls' directorship, to become the person I was destined to be. The mistakes I make these days are far less, because I know my souls' yearning now, and have learnt to trust that voice inside.

Two years later, in 1999, I was in France for a meeting with a client. Yes, I dealt with wine companies internationally who sought my branding and design expertise. This was an

Sacrifice

opportunity to see Michael again as I was departing via London. It was interesting to compare where we were at in our lives. He was still stuck, with the same company, and wearing the same hairy prickly shirt. Interestingly, he had not commited to a relationship, and neither had I. But my life was flourishing with my own self generated prospects: the business was thriving and I'd purchased a larger house so that my boys could live with me, they were 20 and 18 by this stage. When I got on the plane, I knew precisely what to do. I donned the eye mask, placed the headphones on, channelled some classical music.... and sobbed all the way back to Australia. I know that Michael and I had some sort of mystical, even spiritual connection and it was powerful. Whether our meeting was to literally wake our souls up from slumber, he certainly switched on the many components of what it is to be *'human'* for me. I do know this; that LOVE is the answer, to our searching, and our yearning, and that in union with another we become whole.

AUTHORS NOTE

There was never any question of what I would call the book. I knew it before I even wrote it in 1996. On our last night in London, after that euphoric first week together, I awoke suddenly in the night with an epiphany, or such. It was not an inner voice or idea that came from within, it was very exterior, and it was incredibly eerie. I was *told* that I would write a book and to call it *'Sacrifice'*. Perhaps it was my guardian angel? I am not a religious person, but I can only explain the experience as *'devine'*. However it was not until the relationship finally ended that I felt compelled to write it all down. I'd experienced some sort of transcendence within me: the realization that the past is over, and that I had faced my own truth. I also wanted to archive the story for posterity whilst it was fresh - because it was so very special to me and I didnt want time to erode the memories. However it consisted only of Michael's beautiful letters to me, along with my narrative.

After I had finished the Sacrifice manuscript in 1997, I sent it off to my best-friend (Eileen), who said "it was a good story and very publishable."

And to whom I replied, "Well, who is going to want to know about me? I'm not famous!"

So I stuck the manuscript away in my trunk of memorabilia, quite possibly to be read by my children upon my deathbed, just like *'The Bridges of Madison County.'* But the story lay buried in my psyche all these years like a baby wanting to be born, needing an extended period of gestation and a huge bout of that self-belief, before releasing it. When I retired at age 55 and with the intention of exploring my own creative pursuits (instead of designing for others) I thought about the manuscript in the trunk and re-read my story.

I am a different person now from when I first wrote Sacrifice. Upon re-reading my manuscript 18 years on, with the benefit of hindsight, and a few more years of wisdom - I was able to write from a more subjective point of view. The world had become a rapidly changed place, especially with regard to consumer trends and sentiments. My children had grown into adults and even though there has been a plethora of books written during this time that have made erotica quite socially palatable, I still had great difficulty including these. However my reading guinea pigs seemed to like these saucy snippets the most! Even the intimate letters I struggled with releasing. But they were the matrix that our relationship was built upon; they told the story of our love and the complexity of the human condition.

I also needed to ask Michael for my letters back, for inclusion in the book, and for permission to use his. He still had them, hidden away in a box in his attic. I knew somehow that he would not have destroyed the letters. Re-reading my correspondence to him after all that time was a very poignant reminder of how special the relationship was to us both, for all sorts of reasons, the main one of course was finding each other and the personal growth we both developed as a result of our relationship. There is something very soulful about expressing yourself through letter-writing. It becomes a secret code between you both, and the words between us had been crafted very carefully for posterity. Our story and letters remain unchanged and unedited. Although these are only a minor selection of the letters we wrote to each other, I selected only the most relevant to complete the storyline of events.

In March 2013 I received an email from Michael stating that he had been diagnosed with a rare cancer called cholangiocarcinoma (or cancer of the bile duct). He was reaching out to all his friends from down under, that in the event we may be in his neck of the woods to please pay him a a visit. It so transpired that I was indeed visiting London that coming September, so I planned to visit him. He undertook the obligatory Chemotherapy even though the tumor was inoperable. When I met him for lunch, he was incredibly optimistic about life and the future, planning trips to South Africa and Australia the year after. Sadly he did not make it, the tumor returned and the original 13 month prognosis of life expectancy took its toll and he passed away in February 2014.

A strange coincidence happened just when I was embarking on the rewrite of the manuscript. My mother died and we scattered her ashes a year later, when I was almost finished. As I threw the ashes I silently spoke to her, *'This is for you, mum, you and millions of other women like me are the reason why I am about to do this. Please help me with my book.'*

The moment was captured on camera by my son's new partner from England. I had recently given her a card I'd found in San Francisco from my time there, which had sat on my desk for the past 18 years. It is by the artist Richard Stine and titled: *'Woman traversing obstacles by faithfully following her own compass.'* I had purchased it on my last day in San Francisco, looked at it and thought, *Yes!*

I am not sure why I felt compelled to give it away...perhaps it was the fact that she had followed my son out from England, where they had met, and was now living with him in Sydney. After the ceremony, she said, "Barbara, when you threw the ashes, I felt a sense that I had seen the image before, and I think

Sacrifice

it was the card you gave to me." Sure enough (as we later discovered) the angle of my arms and even the position of my hands bears an uncanny resem-blance to the picture on the card. Even the rose petals bear a semblance to the heart on the card— my mother's broken heart finally scattered and laid to rest in the tranquil rock pools of Princess Bay in New Zealand. She had sacrificed her own happiness and stayed with my father for the sake of her family, and she was the reason I had to leave. I wanted my life to matter, to me, and I know she would have applauded me for doing so.

NOTE: This is the 2nd release of Sacrifice. It was first released in 2014 through a traditional publisher. I do love how the World Wide Web has changed the face of traditional publishing; as a result, I have set up my own publishing company titled LIFE IS ART - a non-registered, *name-only* company, and who knows where that might take me? I chose to self-publish for the book's 2nd release, to have more control over the book, as this suits my independent nature. I believe that sharing stories connects us all in a supremely divine way through our real experiences.

If you enjoyed Sacrifice, you can now read my second book, titled - Solitaire [an affair with my heART] – released 2022.

CARPE DIEM

Seize the day - the hour - the moment,
for it is all we have.

SOLITAIRE [an affair with my heART]

This is a highly personal memoir of a woman finding her truth, and coming home to herself through her souls calling to lead a solitary life, albeit a highly creative one. Barbara was renowned for her highly successful graphic design business that was responsible for the inception of the most powerful wine brand in the world - [yellow tail]. However, she relinquished the business for the sake of her spiritual inner health, along with her second marriage and perfectly constructed life. The book will take you on a journey of discovery; illuminating universal concerns of the heart, and exploring questions and actions on what it takes to walk your own path when you feel you are not living your truth.

She states; "From the time we are born we are on a journey. Many of us do not have the luxury of determining which train we will catch, nor which station to either disembark temporarily or where to terminate. In fact, many human beings don't have a lot of choice. So if you have the advantage of *'choice'* in your life, you are fortunate, and I am one of these people. To choose (or not) is akin to Shakespeare saying *'to be, or not to be - that is the question'*. Do we let life carry us along blindly following paths directed for us by our parents and even our own perceptions of a comfortable, but conformed life? We are not all the same, and I am not trying to advocate any sort of doctrine about *'how to conduct a successful life'* or *'manifest your dreams'*. The book is quite simply a compilation of heart-felt chronological short stories created over a 10-year period of my life, and I write in the hope of inspiring others by sharing my gift of art."

Through painting and writing the author reveals her existential questioning, painting her soul's desire and search for a meaningful life. Barbara was also led back to her first husband upon learning of his inoperable brain tumour and went to care for him. It was through this act of compassion that she learned the (inner) art of forgiveness and surrender. Upon this return to one of the most notable and important social constructs of her life, (and the one thing she questioned the most) marriage and companionship gave her all the answers in the end...to *'the game of life' SOLITAIRE!*

AUTHORS NOTE: The book is also a visual account of my paintings which provide an allegorical analysis, defined by Carl Jung's psycho-analytical theories on the archetypal personas as clothing for the soul. I divulge the healing process my creativity brought me through painting my own archetypes and relate how they defined me, through the process of story-telling.

www.ingramcontent.com/pod-product-compliance
Lightning Source LLC
Chambersburg PA
CBHW032105090426
42743CB00007B/240